Decadent
FRUIT DESSERTS

FRESH *and* INSPIRING TREATS *to* EXCITE YOUR SENSES

JACKIE BRUCHEZ, CREATOR *of* THE SEASIDE BAKER

PAGE STREET
PUBLISHING CO.

PAGE STREET
PUBLISHING CO.

First published in 2019 by

Page Street Publishing Co.

27 Congress Street, Suite 105

Salem, MA 01970

www.pagestreetpublishing.com

Distributed by Macmillan, sales in Canada by The Canadian Manda Group.

23 22 21 20 19   1 2 3 4 5

ISBN-13: 978-1-62414-705-0

ISBN-10: 1-62414-705-4

Library of Congress Control Number: 2018951645

Cover and book design by Rosie Stewart for Page Street Publishing Co.

Photography by Jackie Bruchez

Printed and bound in China

TO MY HUSBAND,
KIDS AND GRANDMA.
I LOVE YOU ALL!

Contents

INTRODUCTION

Fruit. It's a food group. It's a lunchbox standard. Easily accessible, no matter where you are in the world. It's readily found in most corner markets, big-box grocery warehouses, farm stands and backyards and patios. Fruit is so ubiquitous that it is often underestimated for its versatility and intense flavor, not to mention its medicinal benefits. Although I have a deep appreciation for fruits in their naked, unsweetened, glorious natural state, I have discovered that fruits shift beautifully into unexpected culinary fare. Fruits transform. That's the idea behind this book. Transforming fruit, be it apples or oranges or more exotic varieties like dragon fruit, into a decadent, sophisticated, blow-your-mind dessert is the revelation I want to share with you.

I'm Jackie, creator of the food blog The Seaside Baker. In addition to my passion for cooking and baking, my family and I love to muck around in our tiny backyard organic farm. It's our skinny slice of heaven that sits atop a bluff, about a mile from the Pacific Ocean. The peek-a-boo ocean view from the roof is lovely, even through the power lines. We have a small flock of spoiled, entitled chickens that think our home is just an extension of their coop. They've taken "free-range" to a whole new level. We had the good fortune of picking a home with over a dozen mature fruit trees. The property is peppered with lemon, orange, fig, pink guava, nectarine, peach, loquat and plum trees. There is a lot of work involved with growing your own food, even on this somewhat small scale. We love it. We really do.

We also visit just about every pick-your-own fruit orchard on the West Coast, and my little ones clean off the trees with the accuracy of agricultural turbine harvesting machines. I always seem to find myself with more fruit than we can possibly eat. My husband often jokes when I come home with too much fruit that we will soon be eating a curd of some sort. Because, after all the pies and cakes are made, there is always more fruit to turn into a delectable fruit curd.

No matter the season, California always has an abundance of beautiful fruit to be enjoyed. Like a kid in a candy store, I often get giddy at the sight of the edible rainbow in front of me at roadside fruit stands and farmers' markets. All that gorgeous deliciousness at its peak freshness! I purchase enough to feed an army. But all that produce will ripen faster than we can eat it, and I was raised with the idiom, "waste not, want not."

Which is reason #322 why I created this cookbook. After years of cooking and baking with fresh produce, I find that adding fresh fruit to a recipe creates a glorious and delicious dessert. It adds color, freshness and, of course, sun-kissed sweetness.

This book is an homage to my life. There are tropical-infused recipes that feature fruits and flavors of Hawaii, where I spent a good part of my childhood. Italian flavors and combinations also are abundant in the book, as this is what I grew up eating at my grandparents' big Sunday dinners. Finally, there are beaucoup French-inspired recipes that have helped manage to keep my husband around for the past fifteen-plus years. They say the way to another's heart is through their stomach, and I can definitely attest to that!

To me, baking is a process that should be enjoyed. When I set out to create a multi-step recipe, I turn the music up and make my kitchen my art studio. Many of my recipes in this book will have a few steps. Fear not. I'm here to walk you through all the steps. For those of you who are more adept in the kitchen, you won't be bored—I promise! So pick a recipe, get set and let's have some fruitin' tootin' fun.

SIMPLY
DRESSED

"Good food is very often, even most often, simple food."

Anthony Bourdain

I am far from simple in everyday life. I've been known to say, "I'll become a minimalist when Elton John does." But when it comes to desserts, sometimes simplicity is key. While I love a good fruit-enhanced cake, I also love a warm and bubbly fruit cobbler. In-season fruits are the best for these sorts of desserts because of their sun-ripened sweetness. This chapter includes recipes from simple Merlot-Poached Pears (page 12) to Blood-Orange Crème Brûlée (page 20). You will find that all the recipes take the tree-ripened fruit to a whole new level and turn them into an elegant dessert perfect for any occasion.

CIDER-BAKED APPLES

Growing up, this is the one dessert that I remember my mom made on a regular basis. It wasn't until well into my adulthood that I began making it for my own family. With a little adapting and some brown sugar butter crumble, these baked apples quickly became a family favorite. Now, it is the first recipe we make after coming home from our annual day of apple picking.

MAKES: 4 apples

Preheat the oven to 350°F (177°C).

To make the cider syrup, pour the cider into a small saucepan over medium heat. Bring it to a simmer, and continue to cook until the cider has reduced to half and is somewhat syrupy, approximately 12 to 15 minutes. Stir in the butter, brown sugar and salt. Pour the syrup into the bottom of an 8 x 8–inch (20 x 20–cm) or 6-cup (1.4-L) baking dish.

To make the crumble filling, in a medium-sized bowl, combine the flour, oats, brown sugar, granulated sugar, salt and cinnamon. Using your fingers or a pastry cutter, cut the cold butter into the flour mixture until pea-sized clumps form. Set it aside.

Cut the tops off the apples. Using a melon baller, core out the center of the apples, leaving about an inch (2.5 cm) of flesh against the skin. Discard the tops, seeds and core, but retain the extra apple flesh. Chop the extra flesh and toss it in with the crumble filling. Brush the insides of the apples with lemon juice to avoid browning. Position the hollow apples in the baking pan over the cider syrup. Fill each apple with the apple-oat crumble filling.

Cover the pan lightly with foil and bake the apples for 20 minutes. Remove the foil and baste the apples with the cider syrup in the baking dish. Bake uncovered for 20 to 30 minutes, depending on the size of the apples. The apples should be soft, but not collapsing.

Serve the apples warm with a scoop of ice cream and drizzle with leftover cider syrup.

CIDER APPLES

2 cups (480 ml) apple cider

2 tbsp (30 g) unsalted butter

3 tbsp (40 g) light brown sugar

¼ tsp salt

CRUMBLE FILLING

½ cup (60 g) all-purpose flour

¼ cup (20 g) rolled oats

⅓ cup (70 g) light brown sugar

¼ cup (50 g) granulated sugar

¼ tsp salt

½ tsp ground cinnamon

4 tbsp (60 g) unsalted butter, chilled and cut into cubes

4 firm cooking apples, such as Granny Smith, Honeycrisp or Braeburn

½ tbsp (8 ml) lemon juice

Vanilla ice cream, for serving

BAKER'S NOTE ~

Apples can also be served with a drizzle of homemade Crème Anglaise (page 53).

MERLOT-POACHED PEARS

Poached pears are one of my favorite desserts to serve at dinner parties during the fall. Like the Cider-Baked Apples (page 11), these pears require little work and a few good quality ingredients. The better the wine you use, the better and more decadent the pears will be.

MAKES: 4 pears

In a medium-sized saucepan, combine the merlot, sugar, vanilla bean, cinnamon stick and cloves over medium-high heat. Bring the mixture to a boil, then reduce the heat and simmer for 5 minutes.

Meanwhile, set out a dish large enough to hold 4 pears. Peel the pears, leaving the stem intact. Cut off the bottoms of the pears to create a flat bottom. Add the pears to the liquid and simmer for 25 minutes, rotating the pears every 5 minutes until they are tender but still somewhat firm. Remove the pears from the liquid and place them on the dish.

Strain the liquid from the saucepan through a fine-mesh sieve into a medium-sized bowl, and then return the liquid to the pan set over medium-high heat. Boil until the liquid has reduced by half, about 15 minutes; cool it to room temperature.

Plate the upright pears on individual serving dishes. Drizzle them with syrup and serve.

3 cups (720 ml) good quality merlot

½ cup (100 g) granulated sugar

1 vanilla bean, cut in half lengthwise

1 whole cinnamon stick

2 whole cloves

4 firm, medium-sized pears, such as Anjou, Bartlett or Bosc

BAKER'S NOTE ～

Poached pears can be made one day ahead. Cover and chill the pears in the strained poaching liquid before reducing the liquid to a syrup. Before serving, separate the pears and liquid and reduce the liquid to a syrup. Rewarm the pears in the syrup over medium-low heat until the pears are warm, if desired. Alternatively, serve the pears at room temperature drizzled with warm syrup.

PUFF PASTRY–BAKED PEARS

A simple yet elegant dessert, these decorative pears are full of rich, deep flavors and a perfectly buttery crust. The juxtaposition of textures from the soft pear and the golden flaky crust will blow your mind.

MAKES: 6 pear halves

Preheat the oven to 400°F (204°C). Line a large baking sheet with parchment paper.

In a small bowl, combine the melted butter, brown sugar, ginger, cinnamon and cardamom; mix well and set it aside.

Unroll the refrigerated puff pastry dough and cut the dough into 6 pear shapes, making the shapes about an inch (2.5 cm) larger than the actual pear. Position the pastry pears on the lined baking sheets 2 inches (5 cm) away from each other. Use the excess pastry to make leaf shapes and attach them to the top of each pear-shaped pastry.

Using a pastry brush, brush the pear-shaped dough and leaves with three-fourths of the butter/sugar mixture. Place the pear halves, core side down, in the center of each pastry. Brush the pears with the remaining butter/sugar mixture.

In a small bowl, whisk the egg and water together. Using the same pastry brush, brush the exposed pastry dough with the egg wash.

Bake for 20 to 30 minutes or until golden brown. Serve them immediately.

3 tbsp (45 ml) unsalted butter, melted

2 tbsp (30 g) light brown sugar

1 tsp fresh ginger, minced

¼ tsp ground cinnamon

¼ tsp ground cardamom

1 sheet puff pastry dough, thawed in the refrigerator overnight

3 pears, peeled, cored and halved

1 whole egg, beaten

2 tbsp (30 ml) water

BAKER'S NOTE

For a French-style dessert, add a small wedge of Brie cheese in the hollowed-out pear core before placing the pears core side down on the pastry.

SUGARED CRANBERRIES

Although cranberries are tart, coating them in sugar makes them a delightful treat and beautiful decoration. I usually make a few bags of these a year and use them on cakes, cookies, salads and cheeseboards. They bring color and a magical visual element to the final dish.

MAKES: 2 cups (200 g)

In a small saucepan, combine the water and granulated sugar over medium heat. Bring it to a simmer, stirring until the sugar dissolves, then remove it from the heat and cool the syrup for 10 minutes.

Place the cranberries in a large bowl and pour the syrup over the top. Stir gently to coat the cranberries with the syrup. Cool them completely, cover them with plastic wrap and refrigerate for at least 2 hours or overnight.

Once the cranberries have steeped and are cold, drain them into a colander. Place the sanding sugar in a shallow dish. Add the cranberries in small batches, rolling to coat them with sugar. Spread the sugared cranberries in a single layer on a parchment-lined baking sheet. Let the cranberries sit at room temperature until dry, about 1 hour. Store the cranberries in an airtight container in a cool, dry place for up to 1 week.

2 cups (480 ml) water

2 cups (400 g) granulated sugar

2 cups (200 g) fresh cranberries

⅔ cup (130 g) sanding sugar

BAKER'S NOTE ~

I usually dip a few sprigs of rosemary in the cranberry syrup before draining the syrup from the cranberries, then I dip the rosemary sprigs in the sugar as well. This also makes for a beautiful decoration, but is not quite edible.

CANDIED KUMQUATS

These slightly tangy yet sweet treats are perfect for nibbling on, garnishing tarts or cakes or even using as a gourmet ice cream topper! They are super simple to make and will keep for up to two months in the refrigerator.

MAKES: 1.5 pints (550 g)

In a medium-sized pot, combine the sugar and water over medium heat; bring it to a simmer.

Slice the kumquats into halves or thirds (for the larger fruits), removing the seeds, if desired. Add the fruit to the simmering syrup and cook for 10 minutes. Remove the pan from the heat and let the fruit steep, covered, for 8 hours.

After the fruit has soaked, return the pan to the stove and bring the syrup to a boil over medium-high heat. Reduce the heat to medium-low and simmer for 10 minutes.

Carefully spoon the fruit and syrup into two half-pint (240-ml), wide-mouth Mason jars and let them cool to room temperature. Once cooled, cover the jars with lids and store them in the refrigerator for up to 2 months.

2 cups (400 g) granulated sugar

1 cup (240 ml) water

1 lb (455 g) whole kumquats, approximately 30–40

BAKER'S NOTE ∿

Leave smaller kumquats whole or cut them in half. Use this recipe to also make candied Meyer lemons. Simply slice four to five Meyer lemons, remove the seeds and proceed with the recipe.

BLOOD-ORANGE CRÈME BRÛLÉE

The first time I had a blood orange was when I was an exchange student in Switzerland. I was still learning my numbers and colors in French, so my host father would bring home different things to teach me new words. Orange was an easy one, because I could simply say it with a French accent. However, when he sliced it open, I gasped, as I had never seen a blood orange before. From then on, this citrus has been one of my favorite ways to glam up a standard dessert or brighten a gloomy winter day.

MAKES: 6 servings

Preheat the oven to 325°F (163°C).

In a heavy-bottomed saucepan, combine the cream, vanilla bean pod and scraped seeds over medium heat. Bring the cream to a low boil, then turn off the heat.

In a medium-sized bowl, whisk the egg yolks and ½ cup (100 g) of the sugar until the mixture is a pale yellow. Whisk in the zest and the blood-orange juice. Temper the egg yolk/orange mixture by very slowly adding the hot cream to the mixture while whisking constantly. Pour the liquid into six (6-oz [180-ml]) ramekins, filling them three-fourths full.

Carefully place the ramekins in a large roasting pan. Fill the roasting pan with enough hot water to come halfway up the sides of the ramekins, being careful not to splash the hot water into the ramekins. Cover the pan with foil. Bake the crème brûlée for 40 to 45 minutes, or until it has set but is slightly jiggly in the center.

Remove the ramekins from the pan and cool them for 10 minutes, then chill them in the refrigerator for at least 2 hours or up to 24 hours.

When you're ready to serve, slice the whole blood orange into six thick slices. Cut off the peel and rind and place an orange slice on each chilled crème brûlée. Sprinkle the ramekins with the remaining ½ cup (100 g) of sugar, then torch the sugar until golden brown. Alternatively, place the ramekins under the broiler set on high. Watch carefully and remove them when the sugar is caramelized.

4 cups (960 ml) heavy cream

1 vanilla bean, split and scraped

6 large egg yolks

1 cup (200 g) granulated sugar, divided

1 tbsp (10 g) blood-orange zest

¼ cup (60 ml) blood-orange juice

1 whole blood orange

BAKER'S NOTE ～

These can also be made in mini 4- or 8-ounce (120- or 140-ml) jars. This is particularly useful when making it for a small crowd because you can cover them with their lids and stack them in the fridge until ready to serve.

STRAWBERRY-RHUBARB ETON MESS

Any name that has the word mess in it resonates with me, despite being an odd name for a dessert. I'm one of those people who thrives in chaos. This dessert may appear to be a bit messy, but it works so well, and the pink-and-white layers contrast beautifully in the glasses! The crunchy meringue pieces absorb the delicious spring compote, and each bite is finished off with a taste of whipped-cream perfection. It's no wonder it has been a staple dessert in England since the late 1800s!

MAKES: 4 servings

In a small saucepan over medium-low heat, combine the rhubarb, 1 cup (160 g) of the strawberries, sugar and lemon juice. Simmer the mixture for about 5 minutes, or until the rhubarb is soft and the strawberries have melted into a syrupy mixture. Remove it from the heat, stir in the remaining ½ cup (80 g) of the strawberries and cool it completely, then refrigerate it until cold, about 1 to 2 hours.

When you're ready to serve, beat the whipping cream and vanilla until stiff peaks form. Dollop a spoonful of the whipped cream into four decorative serving glasses or jars. Sprinkle a few meringue pieces over each glass, then top them with a layer of strawberry-rhubarb compote. Repeat the layers until the glasses are full. Garnish them with fresh strawberry slices and mint leaves, if desired.

1 cup (120 g) rhubarb, diced

1½ cups (240 g) sliced strawberries, divided

½ cup (100 g) granulated sugar

1 tbsp (15 ml) lemon juice

1½ cups (360 ml) heavy whipping cream, cold

1 tsp vanilla extract

8 small meringue cookies, broken into small pieces

4 strawberries, sliced, for garnish, optional

4 sprigs of mint, for garnish, optional

BAKER'S NOTE

The strawberry-rhubarb compote can be made up to two days in advance. Simply stir in the additional ½ cup (80 g) of the fresh strawberries when you're ready to serve.

STRAWBERRY-APRICOT BROWN BUTTER CRUMBLE

There's nothing quite like a fresh, seasonal crumble topped with a giant scoop of melting ice cream. In my husband's hometown in Switzerland, the small highway leading into the village is lined with apricot trees that you can smell from a mile away during the summer. It's something that he reminisces about every year. So whether I'm trying to butter him up before a big purchase or just trying to ease his homesickness, the aroma of this cobbler baking always does the trick.

MAKES: 6 servings

Preheat the oven to 350°F (177°C).

To make the fruit filling, in a deep-dish baking pan sprayed with cooking spray, or three mini cast-iron pans, add the apricots, strawberries, lemon zest, sugar, cornstarch and salt. Gently stir it to evenly coat the fruit; set it aside. If you're using three pans, add the apricots, strawberries, lemon zest, sugar, cornstarch and salt to a large bowl, gently stir it to evenly coat the fruit, then evenly distribute to the three pans.

To make the topping, in a small saucepan, cook the butter over low heat, stirring regularly until the butter is a deep golden color and smells nutty, about 5 to 7 minutes. Remove it from the heat.

In a medium-sized bowl, whisk together the oats, flour, brown sugar, cinnamon and salt. Mix in the browned butter, making sure to scrape the brown bits at the bottom of the pan into the flour mixture.

Sprinkle the crumb topping over the fruit. Bake for 50 to 60 minutes, or until the crisp is golden and bubbling. Allow it to cool for 10 to 15 minutes before serving. Serve with a large scoop of ice cream, if desired.

FRUIT FILLING

8 apricots, peeled and quartered

1 qt (640 g) strawberries, sliced

1 tsp fresh lemon zest

⅓ cup (70 g) granulated sugar

1 tbsp (10 g) cornstarch

¼ tsp salt

TOPPING

¼ cup (60 g) unsalted butter

¾ cup (60 g) old-fashioned rolled oats

¾ cup (100 g) all-purpose flour

⅓ cup (70 g) light brown sugar, packed

¾ tsp ground cinnamon

¼ tsp salt

Ice cream, for serving, optional

BAKER'S NOTE ~

To peel the apricots, mark an X at the bottom of the fruit. Prepare a large bowl of ice water on the side. Bring a large saucepan half-full of water to a boil. Carefully drop the fruit (one to two pieces at a time) into the boiling water and let it sit for 30 to 40 seconds. Remove the fruit with a slotted spoon and submerge it into the ice-cold water for 30 seconds. Remove the fruit from the ice water and gently peel the skin away from the flesh. Cut it in half, remove the pit and slice as desired.

SUMMER BERRY CHAMPAGNE TERRINE

This lovely, refreshing gourmet version of a Jell-O® shot requires no baking and only about fifteen minutes to put together.

MAKES: 6 servings

Mix the gelatin and water in a small bowl; let it sit for 5 minutes.

Line one (9 x 5–inch [23 x 13–cm]) terrine mold or loaf pan with plastic wrap. Arrange the berries inside the pan.

In a medium-sized saucepan set over medium heat, cook the sugar and 1 cup (240 ml) of the champagne until the sugar has dissolved, about 3 minutes. Do not let it boil. Remove it from the heat and add the gelatin mixture. Stir until the gelatin mixture has completely melted into the champagne/sugar mixture. Pour in the remaining 1 cup (240 ml) of champagne, as well as the sparkling grape juice.

Carefully pour the champagne mixture over the berries in the pan, leaving approximately an inch (2.5 cm) of space at the top of the pan. Cover the top of the gelatin with plastic wrap, then cover it with a second terrine or loaf pan, with the bottom of it sitting on the plastic wrap. Place a can from your pantry on top of the second terrine to weigh down the fruit. Refrigerate it overnight.

When you're ready to serve, dip the tin briefly in hot water, then invert it onto a serving plate. Dip a sharp knife into hot water and cut the gelatin mold into slices. Top the servings with extra berries and/or whipped cream.

2 tbsp (30 g) unflavored gelatin

1 cup (240 ml) cold water

2 cups (250 g) berries, plus extra for garnishing

¼ cup (50 g) granulated sugar

2 cups (480 ml) chilled champagne, such as Brut Champagne, divided

1 cup (240 ml) chilled sparkling grape or apple juice

Whipped cream, for garnish

BAKER'S NOTE ⁓

When it comes to berries, I was always taught to secretly test the fruit before buying it. Or for the more socially acceptable route, you can always ask the produce manager in most stores, and they will gladly give you a sample. Make sure the berries are plump, tender and bright in color. Check the bottom of the container for moldy or mushy berries and that the plastic separating the berries from the container is not damp or stained.

HONEY CINNAMON–GRILLED PEACHES

The first time I made these was a few years ago while camping in northern California. I was craving a dessert, and a s'more just wasn't going to cut it. Now, every time we host a backyard BBQ, I always finish the meal with a batch of these. It's the perfect, easy entertaining dessert, as it's gluten free and makes you appear to be healthy, despite the butter and ice cream.

MAKES: 4 servings

Heat the grill to medium-high.

Brush the peach halves with the melted butter and sprinkle them with the cinnamon.

Place the peaches, cut side down, on the grill for about 5 minutes, or when the peaches begin to caramelize and the grill marks appear.

Remove them from the grill. Drizzle a bit of honey over each half and sprinkle them with flaked sea salt. Top the peach halves with a scoop of vanilla bean ice cream. Or add an extra touch by serving them with a scoop of homemade Raspberry-Apricot Mascarpone Ice Cream (page 133).

2 ripe peaches, cut in half and pits removed

2 tbsp (30 ml) unsalted butter, melted

1 tsp ground cinnamon

A drizzle of honey, for garnish

A pinch of flaked sea salt, for garnish

Vanilla bean ice cream, for serving

Raspberry-Apricot Mascarpone Ice Cream (page 133), for serving, optional

BAKER'S NOTE

To peel stone fruit, mark an X at the bottom of the fruit. Prepare a large bowl of ice water on the side. Bring a large saucepan half-full of water to a boil. Carefully drop the fruit (one to two pieces at a time) into the boiling water and let it sit for 30 to 40 seconds. Remove the fruit with a slotted spoon and submerge it into the ice-cold water for 30 seconds. Remove the fruit from the water and gently peel the skin away from the flesh. Cut it in half, remove the pit and slice it as desired. Flash-freeze it on a metal baking sheet until frozen and then transfer them to an airtight bag or container.

STONE FRUIT COBBLER

There's not really anything better in my opinion than warm and bubbling fruit cobbler with a cinnamon-sugar biscuit topping and a giant scoop of vanilla bean ice cream. It is so simple to make, but it hits all of the flavor and texture notes.

MAKES: 6 to 8 servings

Preheat the oven to 375°F (191°C). Lightly spray an 8-inch (20-cm) baking dish or skillet with nonstick cooking spray.

To make the biscuit dough, in a large bowl, sift together the flour, sugar, baking powder and salt. Using your hands or a pastry cutter, cut in the cubed butter to the flour mixture until the mixture is crumbly. Add the buttermilk and stir until it's just combined. There may still be bits of flour, but that's okay. Shape the dough into a disk and wrap it tightly in plastic wrap. Place it in the freezer for 15 minutes or refrigerate it for at least 30 minutes.

To make the fruit filling, in a large bowl, gently toss the peaches, plums, nectarines and cherries with the cornstarch and the vanilla extract. Pour the fruit filling into the baking dish.

On a lightly floured surface, roll out the biscuit dough to a ½-inch (1.5-cm) thickness. Using a 2-inch (5-cm) round cutter, cut the dough into 7 to 8 rounds. Place the dough rounds over the fruit.

For the topping, brush the biscuit dough with the melted butter and then sprinkle it with the sugar and cinnamon.

Bake the cobbler for 20 to 25 minutes or until the biscuits are golden brown and the filling is bubbly. It's best when served warm with a scoop of ice cream.

BAKER'S NOTE

The perfect piece of stone fruit for baking is one that is only slightly soft. Avoid fruit that is bruised or still a bit green around the stem.

BISCUIT TOPPING

1¼ cups (155 g) all-purpose flour

½ cup (100 g) granulated sugar

1 tbsp (12 g) baking powder

1 tsp salt

6 tbsp (80 g) unsalted butter, cold and cubed

½ cup (120 ml) buttermilk

FRUIT FILLING

1 cup (155 g) fresh peaches, peeled and sliced into ¼" (0.6-cm) slices

1 cup (165 g) fresh plums, sliced into ¼" (0.6-cm) slices, peeling is optional

1 cup (140 g) fresh nectarines, sliced into ¼" (0.6-cm) slices, peeling is optional

1 cup (155 g) fresh cherries, pits removed and sliced in half

2 tbsp (20 g) cornstarch

1 tsp vanilla extract

TOPPING

2 tbsp (30 ml) melted butter

1 tbsp (13 g) granulated sugar

¼ tsp ground cinnamon

Ice cream, for serving, optional

PLUM CLAFOUTIS

This simple French custard is elegant and delicious and can be made with just about any fruit. Serve it to friends and introduce it with a French accent, then sit back and enjoy their praises as you secretly smile inside because they have no idea just how easy it was to make.

MAKES: 6 servings

Preheat the oven to 375°F (191°C). Butter a 10-inch (25-cm) baking dish or cast-iron pan, and sprinkle 2 teaspoons (8 g) of sugar over the bottom.

Arrange the plum halves, cut side down, on the bottom of the butter-and-sugar-coated baking dish.

In a blender, combine ½ cup (100 g) of the sugar, as well as the milk, eggs, vanilla, flour and salt. Blend the mixture until smooth, about 2 minutes, then slowly pour it over the fruit.

Bake for 50 to 55 minutes, or until the *clafoutis* is firm and lightly browned. Serve warm or at room temperature. Dust it with powdered sugar before serving, if desired.

BAKER'S NOTE ~

Adjust your sugar to ⅔ cup (130 g), in lieu of the ½ cup (100 g), if your plums are tart and not fully ripe.

1 tbsp (15 g) unsalted butter, room temperature

½ cup (100 g) plus 2 tsp (8 g) granulated sugar, divided

14 Italian plums, sliced in half and pits removed

1¼ cups (300 ml) whole milk

3 large eggs

1 tbsp (15 ml) vanilla extract

⅔ cup (85 g) all-purpose flour

⅛ tsp salt

Powdered sugar, for garnish, optional

HONEY-ROASTED FIGS

Sometimes the best desserts are the simple ones where the ripe fruit can shine. This is one of my favorite late summer/early fall desserts for guests. It is easy to make, beautiful when plated and delicious.

MAKES: 4 to 8 servings

Preheat the oven to 425°F (218°C). Line a baking sheet with foil.

Cut the stems off each fig and cut an X from the top to three-fourths of the way down the middle of the fig. Do not cut all the way to the bottom. Place them on the lined baking sheet.

Heat the honey in a microwave-safe dish for 15 seconds. Stir in the cinnamon and cardamom. Drizzle half of the spiced honey over the figs. Roast the figs for 10 to 12 minutes, or until they are soft and open like a flower.

Scoop 1 tablespoon (8 g) of ricotta into each fig and drizzle them with the remaining spiced honey. Sprinkle the figs with candied pecans and serve immediately.

8 whole Mission figs

⅓ cup (80 ml) honey

¼ tsp ground cinnamon

⅛ tsp ground cardamom

½ cup (65 g) fresh ricotta cheese

Chopped candied pecans, for garnish

BAKER'S NOTE ～

These figs are also delicious served warm on top of a scoop of vanilla bean ice cream. Simply omit the ricotta filling.

FRUITS THAT TAKE *the* CAKE

"Cooking is like painting or writing a song. Just as there are only so many notes or colors, there are only so many flavors—it's how you combine them that sets you apart."

— *Wolfgang Puck*

Incorporating fresh fruit in cakes creates a perfectly paired matrimony of taste and texture. Whether you are sandwiching fresh strawberries between delicate cake layers or baking the fruit right into the batter, it's a delicious way to add a punch of flavor and subtle natural color. It's also a way to glam up a normally boring standard cake with little effort. Too bad getting ready in the morning isn't this easy!

BANANAS FOSTER CAKE

Why settle for simple banana bread when you can have a bite of this outrageously delicious concoction? It may be over the top, but let me tell you, it is worth every second it takes to create and every dish you use doing it. It's one of those cakes that you marvel in glory at after making and must Instagram a picture of once it's done. No filter required.

MAKES: 12 to 15 servings

Preheat the oven to 350°F (177°C). Grease and flour three 8-inch (20-cm) cake pans.

To make the cake, in a medium-sized bowl, combine the flour, baking soda and salt. Set it aside.

In a large bowl, cream the butter, granulated sugar and brown sugar until it's light and fluffy, about 6 minutes. Add the eggs, one at a time, mixing well between additions. Add the mashed banana and vanilla, mixing until they're combined.

In five batches, alternate adding the flour mixture and buttermilk to the butter/sugar mixture, beginning and ending with the flour, mixing on low speed until it's just combined. Scrape down the bowl between additions. Evenly divide the batter between the prepared cake pans. Bake the cakes for 25 to 30 minutes, or until a toothpick is inserted and comes out clean.

To make the fried bananas, bring the butter and brown sugar to a boil in a nonstick frying pan over medium-high heat. Add the banana slices and cook for 2 minutes. Flip the banana slices over and cook for 2 minutes. Remove the pan from the heat and add the rum, if desired. Set the pan aside to cool while making the caramel sauce and the frosting.

(continued)

BANANA CAKE

3 cups (360 g) all-purpose flour

¾ tsp baking soda

½ tsp salt

1½ cups (350 g) unsalted butter, room temperature

1 cup (200 g) granulated sugar

¼ cup (60 g) light brown sugar, packed

3 large eggs

3 medium bananas, mashed

1 tsp vanilla

1½ cups (360 ml) buttermilk, room temperature

FRIED BANANAS

6 tbsp (80 g) unsalted butter

1 cup (240 g) light brown sugar, packed

4 bananas, sliced into thick rounds

3 tbsp (45 ml) dark rum, optional

To make the homemade caramel sauce, heat the brown sugar, heavy cream and salted butter in a heavy-bottomed saucepan over medium-low heat. Whisk gently for about 5 to 7 minutes or until the sauce has thickened. Remove it from the heat and add the vanilla extract. Cool the sauce to room temperature before using.

To make the caramel frosting, beat the butter and caramel sauce together until combined, about 4 minutes. Add the vanilla and half of the powdered sugar and beat until smooth. Add the remaining powdered sugar and 2 tablespoons (30 ml) of the cream and beat on high until it's light and smooth. If the frosting is still stiff, add an additional tablespoon (15 ml) of cream and beat until smooth.

To assemble the cake, cut the domes off of the cakes to level them. Place the first layer on a cake stand. Spread ½ cup (100 g) of the caramel frosting evenly over the surface. Top the frosting with half of the banana slices and about one-third of the sauce. Cover the bananas with the second cake layer and repeat the steps. Once the top layer has been added, frost the top and outside of the cake with the remaining frosting. Drizzle the top edges of the cake with the remaining caramel sauce. The cake can be made and refrigerated 2 days ahead of time. When you're ready to serve, remove the cake from the fridge 1 hour before slicing.

BAKER'S NOTE ~

Make the caramel sauce up to four days ahead of time. Once made, cool the sauce for five minutes, then pour it into a jar to store and refrigerate until ready to use.

CARAMEL SAUCE

1 cup (240 g) light brown sugar, packed

½ cup (120 ml) heavy cream

4 tbsp (60 g) salted butter

1 tsp vanilla extract

CARAMEL FROSTING

¾ cup (180 g) salted butter

¾ cup (180 ml) caramel sauce

1 tsp vanilla extract

5 cups (600 g) powdered sugar, divided

2-3 tbsp (30–45 ml) milk or cream

BLOOD-ORANGE BUNDT CAKE

This is the perfect cake to transition from winter into spring. The winter citrus flavor shines while the vibrant blood-orange colors make for a gorgeous dessert.

MAKES: 10 to 12 servings

To make the candied blood oranges, bring a large pot of water to a boil. Add the orange slices and cook for 1 minute to soften them. In another pot, combine the sugar, orange juice and water over medium heat. Bring the mixture to a boil, stirring constantly until the sugar has dissolved. Reduce the heat to low and add the orange slices. Cook the orange slices until the rind has softened, about 45 minutes, turning them every 15 minutes. Once softened, transfer the slices to a wire rack and cool them for 1 hour. Refrigerate the slices in an airtight container for up to 2 weeks.

To make the cake, preheat the oven to 350°F (177°C). Generously grease and flour a 12-cup (3-L) Bundt cake pan.

Using an electric beater or mixer, cream the butter and sugar until it's light and fluffy, 3 to 5 minutes. Add the eggs, one at a time, incorporating them thoroughly before each addition. Stir in the zest and orange blossom water, if desired.

In a small dish, combine the milk and blood-orange juice.

In a small bowl, whisk together the flour, baking powder and salt.

Add half of the dry ingredients to the butter/sugar mixture, mixing until it's just combined. Add the milk/orange mixture to the butter/sugar mixture, beating until it's just combined. Stir in the remaining dry ingredients, mixing until it's just combined, scraping down the bowl if necessary.

Pour the cake batter into the prepared Bundt cake pan. Bake for 48 to 50 minutes. Cool the cake in the pan for 20 minutes, then turn the cake onto a cooling rack to cool completely.

(continued)

CANDIED BLOOD-ORANGE SLICES

1 blood orange, unpeeled, sliced into ⅛" (0.3-cm) rounds

¾ cup (150 g) granulated sugar

1 tbsp (15 ml) fresh orange juice, either blood-orange juice or regular

2 cups (480 ml) water

BLOOD-ORANGE BUNDT CAKE

1 cup (230 g) unsalted butter, softened

1½ cups (300 g) granulated sugar

4 large eggs

2 tbsp (20 g) blood-orange zest

½ tsp orange blossom water, optional

¾ cup (180 ml) milk

½ cup (120 ml) freshly squeezed blood-orange juice, approximately 4 oranges

3 cups (360 g) all-purpose flour

2 tsp (8 g) baking powder

½ tsp salt

To make the glaze, whisk together the powdered sugar, zest, salt and blood-orange juice until smooth. Pour it over the cooled cake and garnish with candied orange peels.

BAKER'S NOTES ～

When combining the milk and blood-orange juice, the milk may curdle a bit due to the acid, creating a delicious buttermilk.

The cake may have a slightly green tint, especially if there are bits of pulp in the batter. This is because blood oranges contain a class of pigment molecules called anthocyanins. These molecules are sensitive and react to eggs and baking soda. So while the cake tastes amazing, there may be a bit of a green hue.

BLOOD-ORANGE GLAZE

1½ cups (150 g) powdered sugar, sifted

1 tsp blood-orange zest

⅛ tsp salt

3 tbsp (45 ml) freshly squeezed blood-orange juice

TROPICAL FRUIT TRIFLE

This dessert is the grown-up, more organized (pretty layers) and crowd-pleasing sister of the English Eton Mess (page 23). The parents of this delicious edible offspring were the tipsy cake, a cake soaked in brandy, and the Elizabethan Custard, a flavored bowl of almond milk. What I love about this dish, besides it being extremely easy to make, is that there are no rules to making it. You can combine any fruits and flavors you please! This tropical version, however, is one of my favorites because it reminds me of the incredible tropical fruit I used to buy on the side of the road growing up in Hawaii.

MAKES: 10 to 12 servings

Into the bottom of a large, clear bowl or trifle dish, layer half of the cubed angel food cake pieces.

Layer these with half of the Passion Fruit Pastry Cream, one-third of the assorted tropical fruits and one-third of the whipped topping. Repeat until the bowl is full, topping it with whipped topping and tropical fruit.

Refrigerate until ready to serve.

1 (16-oz [453-g]) angel food cake or pound cake, cut into small, bite-sized pieces

1 batch Passion Fruit Pastry Cream, chilled (page 154)

3 cups (750 g) cut-up assorted fresh tropical fruit (papaya, pineapple and kiwi)

16 oz (453 g) whipped topping, such as Cool Whip, thawed

BAKER'S NOTES

When serving, use a large spoon to allow large scoops that keep the trifle somewhat intact. If you don't have time to make the Passion Fruit Pastry Cream (though I highly suggest you do), then instant lemon pudding would be an acceptable substitution.

To flash-freeze excess fruit, cut and prepare the fruit. Place the fruit on a wax- or parchment paper–lined rimmed metal baking sheet so that the fruits are not touching each other. Freeze until they're solid, about two to three hours, and then store them in freezer bags.

RHUBARB-STRIPED MANGO CAKE

While this cake is not really difficult to make, it requires a lot of time and patience. The labor of love is quite visible in the final presentation of this vibrant masterpiece. Each rhubarb strand is shaved and hand-placed on the cake. This is the type of cake that one would make to impress one's future in-laws.

MAKES: 10 to 12 servings

Lightly spray an 8- or 9-inch (20- or 23-cm) springform pan with nonstick cooking spray. Line the bottom of the pan with ladyfingers.

To make the mousse, peel, pit and chop the mangos into large chunks. In a blender, puree the chunks until smooth.

In a small bowl, combine the gelatin and cold water. Allow it to sit and set for 5 minutes.

In a clean, dry bowl, beat the whipping cream and vanilla until stiff peaks form. Set it aside.

Melt the gelatin in the microwave for about 30 seconds. Whisk the gelatin until smooth, and then whisk the mixture into the mango puree. Gently fold the puree into the whipped cream. Pour the mixture into the springform pan and tap it gently on the counter to remove the air bubbles. Cover the pan with plastic wrap and freeze it for at least 4 hours.

Once the cake is frozen, unmold the mousse cake by carefully running a knife around the sides of the pan. Unlock and remove the outer side piece, then place the cake on a serving plate.

To make the rhubarb ribbons, using a mandoline slicer or vegetable peeler, slice or peel the rhubarb stalks to a thickness of about 1/16 inch (0.2 cm).

Place the water and sugar in a small saucepan and bring it to a boil over medium heat. Once boiling, reduce the heat to medium-low so that the syrup is just barely simmering. Add 3 to 4 slices of rhubarb and cook until slightly softened, about 30 seconds. Remove the ribbons from the pan and drain them on paper towels. While the rhubarb ribbons are still warm, lay the strips on top of the mousse until the surface and sides of the cake are completely covered. Trim away the excess ribbons with scissors.

Heat the apricot jam in the microwave for 20 seconds. Using a pastry brush, lightly brush the rhubarb with the warm jam. Freeze the cake for 2 to 3 hours or up to 24 hours. Move it to the refrigerator 1 hour before slicing it with a very sharp knife and serving.

1 (12-oz [340-g]) package ladyfinger cookies

MANGO MOUSSE

2 large mangos

2 tbsp (30 g) unflavored powdered gelatin

6 tbsp (90 ml) cold water

1½ cups (360 ml) heavy whipping cream

1 tsp vanilla extract

RHUBARB RIBBONS

8–10 fresh rhubarb stalks

1 cup (240 ml) water

½ cup (100 g) granulated sugar

½ cup (160 g) apricot jam

BAKER'S NOTE ~

If ladyfingers are not available, substitute them with a 12-ounce (340-g) pound cake cut into slices and layered into the bottom of the pan.

FRESH RASPBERRY-LIME CAKE

This raspberry-studded lime cake paired with fruity pink frosting is pretty much the only thing I want to eat during the summer. Since it is already bathing suit season, I decided that instead of getting into swimsuit shape, I'd best shift my focus on getting into swimsuit cover-up shape and enjoy another slice.

MAKES: 10 to 12 servings

Preheat the oven to 350°F (177°C). Prepare three 6-inch (15-cm) or two 8-inch (20-cm) cake pans by lining the bottoms with parchment paper rounds and greasing the sides of the cake pans.

In a small bowl, gently toss the raspberries in 2 teaspoons (6 g) of flour; set them aside.

To make the cake, in the bowl of your mixer, whisk together the flour, sugar, baking soda and salt. Create a well in the center and add the milk, lime zest, lime juice, oil, eggs and egg white. Beat until it's just combined. Evenly pour the batter into the cake pans. Press the raspberries into the batter. Bake 6-inch (15-cm) cakes for 20 to 22 minutes and 8-inch (20-cm) cakes for 23 to 26 minutes or until a toothpick is inserted and comes out clean. Remove the cakes from the oven and allow them to cool for 5 minutes. Remove the cakes from the pans and place them on a cooling rack to cool completely.

To make the frosting, in the bowl of your mixer, beat together the butter and cream cheese. Add the raspberry jam, lime juice, lime zest and salt and beat until they're combined. Slowly add half of the powdered sugar; beat until it's smooth. Add the remaining powdered sugar and beat until it's smooth and fluffy.

Place the first layer of the cake on a serving plate. Spread an even layer of the frosting onto the cake layer. Repeat with the remaining layers. Frost the outside of the cake with the remaining frosting. Just before serving, top the cake with fresh raspberries and lime wedges.

BAKER'S NOTE

Make the cake portion of this recipe up to three days in advance by tightly wrapping the cooled cake layers individually in plastic wrap and freezing them. Defrost the cake layers for one hour before icing them.

CAKE

1 cup (130 g) fresh raspberries, plus more for garnish

2½ cups (343 g) cake flour, plus 2 tsp (6 g) for coating raspberries

2 cups (400 g) sugar

¾ tsp baking soda

1 tsp salt

1 cup (240 ml) whole milk

2 tsp (6 g) lime zest

¼ cup (60 ml) lime juice

½ cup (120 ml) vegetable oil

2 eggs plus 1 egg white

FROSTING

½ cup (120 g) unsalted butter, room temperature

4 oz (113 g) cream cheese, room temperature

¼ cup (80 g) seedless raspberry jam

1 tbsp (15 ml) lime juice

2 tsp (6 g) lime zest

¼ tsp salt

3 cups (360 g) powdered sugar

Lime wedges, for garnish

MEYER LEMON CHIFFON CAKE

If you are a lemon lover, you are going to fall head over heels for this cake. With its sweet lemon-y cake base and tart glaze, it's the perfect burst of lemon sunshine!

MAKES: 12 servings

Preheat the oven to 325°F (163°C). Generously grease a 12-cup (3-L) tube pan with nonstick cooking spray.

To make the cake, in a large bowl, sift together the cake flour, ¾ cup (150 g) sugar, baking powder and salt. Create a well in the center of the flour. Pour the oil, egg yolks, milk, lemon juice and zest into the center of the well. With an electric mixer, beat the flour mixture and wet ingredients until they're just combined. Do not overbeat.

In a separate bowl, beat the egg whites with clean beaters until frothy. Once frothy, add the remaining sugar and cream of tartar and beat it until stiff peaks form, about 5 minutes.

Using a rubber spatula, gently fold half of the whites into the batter until it's almost fully incorporated. Add the remaining whites and gently fold until it's combined. Pour the batter evenly into the tube pan.

Bake for 50 to 55 minutes or until the top of the cake springs back when touched. Allow the pan to cool for 5 minutes, then invert the pan over a wire rack and allow it to cool for 1 hour upside down. If the cake has not yet released from the pan, gently run a knife around the edges to loosen it. Cool it completely.

To make the glaze, combine the sifted powdered sugar, heavy cream, lemon juice and zest with a whisk until smooth. Pour it over the cooled cake, then slice and serve.

CHIFFON CAKE

2¼ cups (310 g) cake flour

1½ cups (300 g) granulated sugar, divided

2¼ tsp (10 g) baking powder

½ tsp salt

½ cup (120 ml) vegetable oil

7 large eggs, separated

¾ cup (180 ml) whole milk

¼ cup (60 ml) Meyer lemon juice

1 tbsp (10 g) Meyer lemon zest

½ tsp cream of tartar

LEMON GLAZE

2 cups (200 g) powdered sugar, sifted

1 tbsp (15 ml) heavy cream

2 tbsp (30 ml) Meyer lemon juice

1 tbsp (10 g) Meyer lemon zest

BAKER'S NOTE ⌀

If you do not have cake flour, simply measure out 1 cup (120 g) of regular all-purpose flour and remove 2 tablespoons (15 g). Add 2 tablespoons (20 g) of cornstarch to the flour and sift it. For this particular recipe, you will need to remove 4½ tablespoons (40 g) from 2¼ cups (290 g) of all-purpose flour and add 4½ tablespoons (45 g) of cornstarch to the remaining flour.

QUICK RHUBARB CAKE *with* CRÈME ANGLAISE

This is by far one of the most popular recipes on my site. The recipe was passed down to me from my husband's grandmother. In French, the recipe is called gateau vite fait, which translates to quick cake. True to its name, it takes only a few minutes to prepare.

MAKES: 8 servings

Preheat the oven to 350°F (177°C). Grease and flour an 8- or 9-inch (20- or 23-cm) cake pan.

To make the cake, in a large bowl, beat the eggs and ⅔ cup (130 g) of the sugar until light, about 3 minutes. Beat in the melted butter, milk and vanilla. Stir in the flour, baking powder and salt; mix it to combine. Pour the batter into the cake pan.

Spread the diced rhubarb around the top of the batter and sprinkle it with 2 tablespoons (25 g) of sugar. Bake for 30 minutes or until a knife comes out clean.

To make the crème anglaise, combine the milk and cream in a heavy-bottomed saucepan on medium-high heat; bring it to a simmer, then remove it from the heat.

In a separate bowl, whisk the egg yolks and sugar until it's pale. Temper the yolk mixture by gradually whisking small amounts at a time of the hot milk mixture into the yolk mixture.

Return the custard to the saucepan. Stir it over low heat until the custard thickens and coats the back of a spoon, about 5 minutes. Remove the pan from the heat and stir in the vanilla. For a smooth finish, and to remove clumps, strain the sauce through a fine-mesh sieve into a bowl, if desired. Cover and chill it until ready to use.

Drizzle the sauce over the rhubarb cake slices right before serving.

BAKER'S NOTE

This rhubarb cake is a great recipe for people with allergies. It is extremely versatile, and the flour and milk can be substituted with gluten-free flour and nut or coconut milk.

CAKE

3 large eggs

⅔ cup (130 g) granulated sugar, plus 2 tbsp (25 g) for on top of rhubarb

3 tbsp (45 ml) unsalted butter, melted

2 tbsp (30 ml) milk or buttermilk

1 tsp vanilla extract

1 cup plus 2 tbsp (135 g) all-purpose flour

¾ tsp baking powder

¼ tsp salt

2 cups (240 g) rhubarb, diced

CRÈME ANGLAISE

½ cup (120 ml) milk

½ cup (120 ml) heavy whipping cream

3 large egg yolks

3 tbsp (40 g) sugar

1 tsp vanilla extract

NO-BAKE MINI CHEESECAKES

These are the perfect little desserts to make and take. They come together in less than twenty minutes (plus chilling time) and are perfectly portable and bursting with berry flavor. It's a mother's potluck dream recipe! The best thing about it is that you don't even have to turn on the oven!

MAKES: 12 servings

Remove the lids and rims from 12 (4-ounce [113-g]) jars.

To make the crust, in a small bowl, toss together the ground graham cracker crumbs, brown sugar and melted butter until the mixture is moist. Firmly press about a tablespoon (6 g) of the crust mixture into the bottom of each 4-ounce (113-g) jar.

To make the filling, in a small microwave-safe bowl, sprinkle the gelatin over the water; let it sit until firm.

In a food processor or blender, pulse the strawberries, blueberries and raspberries until they're coarsely chopped.

In a large bowl, beat the cream cheese until light and fluffy. Gradually add the sweetened condensed milk and berry mixture; beat until it's smooth. Microwave the gelatin for 15 to 20 seconds until it's melted. Pour the gelatin into the cream cheese mixture and beat thoroughly to combine them, about 2 minutes on high. Stir in the lemon juice and vanilla. Pour the cheesecake filling over the crusts. Cover the jars with lids and refrigerate for at least 2 hours or up to 2 days. When you're ready to serve, garnish with whipped cream and extra berries.

BAKER'S NOTE ~

These can also be made in six (8-ounce [226-g]) wide-mouth jars or one large 9-inch (23-cm) springform pan.

GRAHAM CRACKER CRUST

1½ cups (125 g) graham cracker crumbs, about 10 to 12 full graham crackers

2 tbsp (30 g) light brown sugar

½ cup (120 g) unsalted butter, melted

BERRY CHEESECAKE FILLING

1 (¼-oz [7-g]) packet unflavored gelatin

¼ cup (60 ml) cold water

¼ cup (40 g) strawberries, washed, dried and stems removed

¼ cup (25 g) blueberries, washed and dried

¼ cup (35 g) raspberries, washed and dried

2 (8-oz [226-g]) blocks of cream cheese, room temperature

1 (14-oz [397-g]) can of sweetened condensed milk

1 tbsp (15 ml) lemon juice

1 tsp vanilla extract

Whipped cream and extra berries, for garnish

BLUEBERRY-THYME POUND CAKE

I love adding fresh herbs to baked goods—especially thyme. Thyme adds a subtle dry aroma, with minty undertones, which adds just the right hint of flavor to this decadent fruity pound cake. Fresh herbs and edible flowers are a great way to glam up a dessert too. The greens from the herbs pair perfectly with the deep purple and sometimes green interior of the blueberry. Bonus points if your thyme bush is in blossom and you can garnish with its gorgeous lilac-colored blossoms.

MAKES: 8 servings

Preheat the oven to 350°F (177°C). Spray a 9 x 5-inch (23 x 13-cm) loaf pan with nonstick cooking spray or line it with aluminum foil.

To make the pound cake, in a small bowl, whisk together the flour, baking powder and salt; set it aside.

Beat the butter and sugar until light and fluffy. Add the eggs and vanilla and beat until combined. Alternatively add the flour mixture and the buttermilk in two parts to the butter mixture. Stir in the thyme and blueberries.

Spoon the batter into the loaf pan. Bake for approximately 50 minutes or until the top is a golden brown and a toothpick inserted into the middle comes out clean. Place the pan on a wire rack to cool completely.

To make the glaze, combine the powdered sugar, blueberries and lemon zest in a food processor and pulse until smooth. Strain it through a sieve for an extra smooth finish, if desired. Pour the glaze over the cooled cake and let it set for 20 minutes before serving.

POUND CAKE

1½ cups (180 g) all-purpose flour

2 tsp (8 g) baking powder

½ tsp salt

¾ cup (180 g) unsalted butter, room temperature

1½ cups (300 g) granulated sugar

3 large eggs

½ tsp vanilla extract

⅓ cup (80 ml) buttermilk, room temperature

½ tsp fresh thyme, chopped

1 cup (100 g) blueberries

GLAZE

1 cup (130 g) powdered sugar

¼ cup (25 g) blueberries

1 tsp lemon zest

BAKER'S NOTES ~

Yogurt can be used in place of the buttermilk in this recipe.

If you do not have a food processor to make the glaze, simply cook the blueberries, lemon zest and 1 tablespoon (15 ml) of water until the blueberries begin to pop. Mash the blueberries, then strain them through a sieve. Whisk in the powdered sugar until smooth.

The BEST REAL STRAWBERRY CAKE

If there ever was a cake that encased the true flavors of spring or summer, this cake would be it. The deep fruity flavor comes from a bit of labor, but is oh so worth it.

MAKES: 12 to 15 servings

To make the cake, in a small saucepan over medium-low heat, cook the strawberry puree, stirring occasionally. When the mixture begins to bubble, reduce the heat to low. Simmer for about 30 minutes, stirring occasionally, or until the mixture has reduced down to about ¾ cup (180 ml). Remove it from the heat and cool it to room temperature. If not using it right away, refrigerate the puree.

Preheat the oven to 350°F (177°C). Grease and flour three 8-inch (20-cm) cake pans or two 9-inch (23-cm) cake pans. Combine the cake flour, baking soda and salt in a bowl; set it aside.

Beat the butter and sugar on high until smooth and creamy, about 5 minutes. Scrape down the sides of the bowl, then add the whole eggs and egg whites. Beat it on high for 3 minutes. Stir in the vanilla extract. Combine the cooled, condensed strawberry puree and buttermilk. With the mixer running on low, alternatively add the flour mixture and the strawberry-buttermilk mixture to the batter in two additions, mixing only until it's just combined. Do not overmix.

Divide the batter evenly into the pans and lightly tap the bottom of the pans to remove air bubbles. Bake 8-inch (20-cm) cakes for 20 to 22 minutes and 9-inch (23-cm) cakes for 22 to 25 minutes or until a toothpick is inserted and comes out clean. Remove them from the oven and allow the cakes to cool completely in the pans on a wire rack. Once cooled, remove them from the pans.

To make the frosting, pulse the freeze-dried strawberries in a food processor or blender until finely crushed. Pour it into a mixing bowl, and add the butter and cream cheese. Beat it on high for 3 minutes until light and creamy. Scrape down the sides of the bowl and add the powdered sugar, heavy whipping cream, vanilla and salt, mixing on low until it's combined. Once combined, increase the mixer speed to high and beat it for 4 to 5 minutes.

To assemble the cake, use a large serrated knife to remove the domes and level the cake. Place the first layer of cake on a serving platter or cardboard cake circle. Spread 1 cup (200 g) of frosting evenly over the cake. Top this with the next layer and repeat the process. Frost the outside of the cake with the remaining frosting and garnish with fresh strawberries, if desired.

CAKE

2 cups (480 ml) fresh strawberry puree

3 cups (410 g) cake flour

1 tsp baking soda

½ tsp salt

1 cup (230 g) unsalted butter, softened

2 cups (400 g) granulated sugar

2 whole large eggs

2 large egg whites

2 tsp (10 ml) vanilla extract

½ cup (120 ml) buttermilk, room temperature

FROSTING

2 cups (450 g) freeze-dried strawberries

1 cup (230 g) unsalted butter, softened

½ cup (115 g) cream cheese, softened

6 cups (720 g) powdered sugar

5 tbsp (75 ml) heavy whipping cream

2 tsp (10 ml) vanilla extract

⅛ tsp salt

Fresh strawberries, for garnish, optional

PLUM CORNMEAL UPSIDE-DOWN CAKE

Growing up, the only cornmeal I had ever had was the kind that we made from the twenty-five-cent boxes that turned into cornbread. I loved it, despite needing a gallon of water after swallowing a bite. It wasn't until I traveled to Texas that I had my first really, really good slice of cornbread. Since then, I have learned to make a great homemade version and even expanded my cornmeal recipe arsenal. This is a great cake because it is easy to make and the beautiful plums decorate the cake. Their juices cook into the cornmeal base, making it extra delicious! Make it with the plums first, then try it again with peaches. Both are so delicious!

MAKES: 10 servings

Preheat the oven to 350°F (177°C). Grease and flour a 9-inch (23-cm) cake pan.

For the fruit, melt the butter and pour it into the baking pan. Sprinkle it with brown sugar. Arrange the plum slices in a single layer over the brown sugar.

For the cake, in a small bowl, whisk together the flour, cornmeal, baking powder, baking soda and salt. Set it aside.

In a large bowl, beat the buttermilk, brown sugar, oil, eggs and vanilla until smooth. Pour the combined wet ingredients into the flour mixture and mix until they're just combined. Spoon the batter over the plums.

Bake for 45 to 50 minutes or until a toothpick inserted in the center comes out clean. Cool it for 10 minutes before inverting it onto a serving plate. For the best results, serve it warm with a scoop of ice cream or cream and a drizzle of honey.

BAKER'S NOTE ～

Full-fat buttermilk is one of my absolute favorite ingredients. It adds so much moisture and flavor to baked goods. However, it's not a common ingredient to have on hand. To make a homemade version, measure out 1 scant cup (240 ml) of whole milk. Stir in 1 tablespoon (15 ml) of lemon juice or white vinegar and let it stand for 5 to 10 minutes. Make sure the homemade buttermilk is at room temperature (unless otherwise stated), then proceed with the recipe.

FRUIT

4 tbsp (60 g) unsalted butter

¼ cup (60 g) light brown sugar, packed

4-5 plums, pitted and sliced into wedges

CORNMEAL CAKE

1 cup (120 g) all-purpose flour

½ cup (80 g) fine cornmeal

1 tsp baking powder

¼ tsp baking soda

¼ tsp salt

1 cup (240 ml) buttermilk, room temperature

½ cup (120 g) light brown sugar, packed

⅓ cup (80 ml) vegetable oil

2 large eggs

1 tsp vanilla extract

Ice cream, for serving, optional

Cream, for serving, optional

Drizzle of honey, for serving, optional

FRESH FIG BANANA BREAD

For about a month every summer, our diets consist of sweet fresh figs and an abundance of fig-enhanced desserts and jams. Like the book, Blueberries for Sal, *I often find my youngest son leaning against the trunk of the fig tree covered in sweet juice and eating his weight in fresh figs. He has become the master at picking the fruit at its prime. After my family has had their fill of the fresh figs, I begin picking them and turning them into something we can enjoy later. Apart from the jars and jars of jam that I make, I usually make a few loaves of this delicious bread to freeze for quick snacks when the school year begins.*

MAKES: 1 standard-sized loaf

Preheat the oven to 350°F (177°C). Line a 9 x 5-inch (23 x 13-cm) loaf pan with parchment paper or foil or spray it with nonstick cooking spray.

In a small bowl, whisk together the flour, baking soda and salt; set it aside.

Beat the butter and sugar together. Add the mashed bananas, egg and vanilla, beating until they're combined. Stir in the flour mixture. Fold in the chopped figs. Pour the batter into the loaf pan and top it with sliced figs. Bake the loaf for 55 to 60 minutes or until a knife inserted in the center comes out clean. Remove it from the oven and cool before slicing.

BAKER'S NOTE ∿

If freezing it for later, wrap the cooled loaf tightly in plastic wrap. Store the wrapped loaf in a freezer bag for up to three months. Bring it to room temperature before serving.

1½ cups (180 g) all-purpose flour

1 tsp baking soda

¼ tsp salt

⅓ cup (80 ml) unsalted butter, melted

¾ cup (150 g) granulated sugar

2–3 very ripe medium-sized bananas, peeled and mashed

1 large egg

1 tsp vanilla extract

1½ cups (225 g) fresh black or Mission figs, chopped

2 whole figs, sliced, for garnish

SURPRISE PEAR GINGERBREAD

Growing up, I loved surprises. It didn't matter if they were big or small. As an adult, I am more of the person who creates the surprises rather than receives them. So when I cut into a loaf of delicious gingerbread and find that there are hidden halved pears inside, my inner child goes a bit nuts. It's a bit strange, seeing as how I know that the pears are there, well, because I put them there. Oh well, we all have our quirks.

MAKES: 8 servings

Peel the pears and cut ½ inch (1.3 cm) off the bottom so that the pear can stand up straight. Slice the pears in half and core out the center.

To make the poached pears, in a large saucepan, combine the water, sugar, cinnamon stick, cloves and ginger over medium heat. Bring the mixture to a boil, then reduce the heat to a simmer and add the halved pears. Cover and simmer it for 20 to 25 minutes or until the pears are tender. Remove the pears from the liquid. Discard the liquid. Set the pears aside to cool.

To make the gingerbread loaf, preheat the oven to 350°F (177°C). Grease or line a 9 x 5 x 3-inch (23 x 13 x 8-cm) loaf pan; set it aside.

In a large bowl, sift together the flour, baking soda, ginger, cinnamon, cloves, allspice and salt; set it aside.

Using a mixer or electric beater, cream the butter, sugar and molasses until it's well combined. Add the egg and vanilla; mix well. Gradually add the flour mixture, mixing until it's just combined. Stir in the hot water. Pour the batter into the loaf pan, then gently press the pears, bottom sides down, into the batter, leaving the stems slightly exposed.

Bake the loaf for 45 to 50 minutes or until a knife is inserted and comes out clean. Cool it completely on a wire rack before slicing. Dust it with powdered sugar before serving, if desired.

BAKER'S NOTE ~

To make a drunken surprise gingerbread loaf, replace the water in the poaching process with a bottle of chardonnay.

POACHED PEARS

3 pears (Bosc, Anjou or Barlett work well)

1 qt (950 ml) water

1⅓ cups (270 g) granulated sugar

1 cinnamon stick

1 tsp whole cloves

½ tsp fresh ginger, 2–3 thin slices

GINGERBREAD LOAF

2 cups (240 g) all-purpose flour

1 tsp baking soda

¾ tsp ground ginger

1 tsp ground cinnamon

⅓ tsp ground cloves

¼ tsp allspice

⅓ tsp salt

6 tbsp (80 g) unsalted butter, softened to room temperature

⅓ cup (70 g) granulated sugar

¾ cup (180 ml) dark molasses

1 large egg

1 tsp pure vanilla extract

¾ cup (180 ml) hot water

1 tbsp (8 g) powdered sugar, for serving, optional

APPLE CAKE *with* APPLE BUTTER FILLING *and* DULCE *de* LECHE FROSTING

Half the nation gets excited when pumpkin spice lattes are released, but in my house, that fall excitement comes from this apple cake. Fall is one of our favorite times of the year, because it means Halloween and the beginning of my family's birthday season is just around the corner. We have birthdays or major holidays every two weeks beginning mid-October through the end of January. So, this cake is like our fall inauguration celebration. If this cake is on the table, it means that the season of fun and celebration has begun.

MAKES: 12 to 15 servings

To make the *dulce de leche*, place the unopened can of sweetened condensed milk in the bottom of your slow cooker. Fill the slow cooker with water until it's about 2 inches (5 cm) above the can. Set the slow cooker to low and cook for 8 hours. Once done, carefully remove the can from the water and set it aside to cool completely.

To make the cake, begin by preheating the oven to 350°F (177°C). Grease and flour three 8-inch (20-cm) or two 9-inch (23-cm) round cake pans.

Grate the peeled apples using a metal cheese grater. Place them in a bowl and toss with lemon juice; set it aside.

In a small bowl, whisk together the flour, allspice, cinnamon, baking powder and soda and salt; set it aside.

In a large bowl, beat the softened butter, brown sugar, granulated sugar and oil until it's well incorporated, about 5 minutes.

(continued)

HOMEMADE DULCE DE LECHE

1 (14-oz [397-g]) can sweetened condensed milk

½ gallon (2 L) water, approximately

APPLE CAKE

3 medium-sized apples (Granny Smith, Honeycrisp or Braeburn), peeled and cored

1 tbsp (15 ml) lemon juice, fresh or bottled

2¼ cups (290 g) all-purpose flour

½ tsp allspice

1 tsp ground cinnamon

1 tsp baking powder

¼ tsp baking soda

½ tsp salt

¾ cup (180 g) unsalted butter, room temperature

1 cup (240 g) light brown sugar, packed

½ cup (100 g) granulated sugar

¾ cup (180 ml) vegetable oil

Add the eggs and vanilla; mix until it's combined.

With the mixer running on low, gradually add the flour mixture, mixing until it's only just combined. Fold in ¼ cup (60 ml) of the homemade dulce de leche to the cake batter, mixing until it's only just combined.

Divide the batter evenly into the pans. Slightly tap them to remove air bubbles. Bake 8-inch (20-cm) cakes for 20 to 22 minutes and 9-inch (23-cm) cakes for 22 to 25 minutes or until a knife inserted in the center comes out clean. Remove them from the oven and allow the cakes to cool completely in the pans on a wire cooling rack. Once cooled, remove the cakes from the pans.

To make the meringue frosting, combine the egg whites and brown sugar in a clean glass bowl over a pan of simmering hot water. Whisk the mixture constantly until the brown sugar has dissolved and is no longer grainy and the mixture is warm to the touch. Transfer the mixture to a stand mixer fitted with a whisk attachment and beat the whites until stiff peaks form and it is no longer warm. Switch to the paddle attachment and gradually add the softened salted and unsalted butter cubes. Once all the butter has been added, add ¼ cup (60 ml) of homemade dulce de leche and the vanilla. Increase the mixer speed to high and mix for 10 minutes or until the frosting is smooth. Spoon the frosting into a large pastry bag.

To assemble the cake, trim the tops of the cakes using a serrated knife to create a level surface and place one layer on a cake stand.

Pipe a round of frosting along the outer edge of the cake layer to create a dam. Spread a thick layer of apple butter inside the frosting, then top it with a light layer of frosting over the apple butter. Repeat with the following layers.

Once the cake has been filled and stacked, frost the top and outside of the cake. Refrigerate it for 1 hour before serving.

If you're topping it with additional homemade dulce de leche, heat ¼ cup (60 ml) of the homemade dulce de leche in a microwave-safe bowl for 15 to 30 seconds or until it is smooth but not hot. Drizzle it onto the cold cake.

APPLE CAKE (CONTINUED)

3 large eggs

1 tsp vanilla extract

¼ cup (60 ml) homemade dulce de leche

DULCE DE LECHE SWISS MERINGUE

3 large egg whites

¾ cup (170 g) light brown sugar, firmly packed

¾ cup (180 g) unsalted butter, cubed and softened

¾ cup (180 g) salted butter, cubed and softened

½ cup (60 ml) homemade dulce de leche, divided

1 tsp vanilla extract

1–2 cups (280–560 g) apple butter

TIGER FIG PISTACHIO ROULADE

Tiger figs are one of the most stunning pieces of fruit and make for a showstopping dessert. Their bright yellow-and-green-striped exterior paired with the vibrant pink interior make them the best cake decoration. Paired with pistachios, honey and mascarpone, this late summer dessert is a keeper!

MAKES: 8 to 10 servings

Preheat the oven to 350°F (177°C). Grease and flour the edges of a large (17 x 12-inch [43 x 30-cm]) rimmed baking pan, and line the bottom of the pan with parchment paper.

Using a food processor or blender, pulse the pistachios and 2 tablespoons (25 g) of the granulated sugar until finely ground, resembling a sandy mixture.

To make the cake, in a medium-sized bowl, whisk together the cake flour, baking powder, salt and ground pistachios; set it aside.

In a separate bowl, beat together the egg yolks, 2 tablespoons (25 g) of the granulated sugar, vanilla and melted butter with an electric mixer for about 5 minutes, or until the mixture is a pale yellow. Stir in the flour mixture.

In a dry, clean bowl, beat the egg whites and cream of tartar on medium speed until soft peaks form. Add the remaining ¼ cup (50 g) of sugar and beat on high until stiff peaks form.

Fold the egg whites, one-third at a time, into the batter, until all the egg whites have been folded in. Spread the batter evenly into the prepared baking pan.

Bake for 15 to 18 minutes, or until the cake is golden brown and springs back when lightly touched in the center.

Sift the powdered sugar onto a large, clean dish towel. Remove the cake from the oven and carefully flip it over onto the dish towel and remove the parchment paper. Starting with the short end, roll the hot cake with the dish towel inside. Set it aside to cool completely, about 30 minutes.

(continued)

PISTACHIO CAKE

¾ cup (95 g) pistachios, roasted, unsalted

½ cup (100 g) granulated sugar, divided

¾ cup (100 g) cake flour

¾ tsp baking powder

¼ tsp salt

8 large eggs, separated

1 tsp vanilla extract

3 tbsp (45 ml) unsalted butter, melted then cooled slightly

½ tsp cream of tartar

3 tbsp (25 g) powdered sugar

To make the filling, in a medium-sized bowl, beat the cheese, sugar, honey and cream until smooth. Unroll the cooled pistachio cake, and evenly spread the filling over the cake. Sprinkle the cake with the chopped figs. Reroll the cake, starting with the short end. Place the cake on a serving platter, cover it loosely and refrigerate until you're ready to serve.

Once you're ready to serve, trim the edges, sift the powdered sugar over the cake and garnish it with fresh figs, pistachios and a drizzle of honey.

BAKER'S NOTE ~

If not serving it the same day, wrap the cake log tightly in plastic wrap and twist the edges like a candy wrapper. Refrigerate it for up to 48 hours.

HONEY MASCARPONE FILLING

12 oz (340 g) mascarpone cheese, room temperature

¾ cup (90 g) powdered sugar

¼ cup (60 ml) honey

2 tbsp (30 ml) heavy cream

4-5 Tiger figs, stems removed and coarsely chopped

GARNISH

1 tbsp (8 g) powdered sugar

4-5 Tiger figs, sliced in half or quartered

1 tbsp (9 g) roasted pistachios

2 tsp (10 ml) honey

CRANBERRY-ORANGE BUNDT CAKE

If you follow my blog, The Seaside Baker, you will find that there are quite a few Bundt cakes in the recipe archives. A Bundt cake is my go-to cake recipe when I'm short on time because the pan basically decorates the cake for you. This particular cake is a holiday staple in my home. It has all of the delicious flavors of winter, and the toppings are bright and festive.

MAKES: 12 to 15 servings

Preheat the oven to 350°F (177°C). Grease and flour a 12-cup (3-L) Bundt pan.

To make the cake, in a medium-sized bowl, whisk together the flour, salt, baking powder and soda; set it aside.

In a mixing bowl, cream the butter and sugar until it's light and airy. Mix in the eggs, one at a time, incorporating it thoroughly before each addition. Stir in the zest.

In a separate bowl, combine the buttermilk and orange juice.

Alternatively add the flour mixture and buttermilk to the butter/sugar mixture in five additions. Fold in the cranberries and white chocolate. Transfer the batter into the Bundt pan.

Bake for 45 to 50 minutes or until the top is golden brown and a knife inserted in the center comes out clean. Cool the pan on a wire rack for 10 minutes, then invert it to remove the cake and cool it for 30 minutes.

To make the ganache glaze, pour the white chocolate into a bowl. Microwave the heavy cream in a microwave-safe bowl for 20 to 30 seconds, or until it's hot. Pour the hot cream over the bowl of white chocolate chips. Let it stand for 5 minutes, then stir until it's smooth. If needed, microwave the ganache for 10 seconds at a time, stirring gently between intervals, until it's smooth. Pour the ganache over the cooled cake while it's on the cooling rack so the excess doesn't pool at the bottom. Allow the ganache to set for 30 minutes, then carefully transfer the cake to a serving plate. Garnish it with Sugared Cranberries and orange slices, if desired.

BAKER'S NOTE ~

This cake can also be made into two loaf pans. Adjust the baking time to 30 to 35 minutes.

CAKE

3 cups (360 g) all-purpose flour

½ tsp salt

1½ tsp (6 g) baking powder

½ tsp baking soda

1 cup (230 g) unsalted butter, room temperature

1½ cups (300 g) granulated sugar

4 large eggs

1 tbsp (10 g) freshly grated orange zest

1 cup (240 ml) buttermilk, room temperature

2 tbsp (30 ml) orange juice

1½ cups (150 g) fresh cranberries

1 cup (170 g) white chocolate chips

WHITE CHOCOLATE GLAZE

1 cup (170 g) white chocolate chips or chopped white chocolate

¼ cup (60 ml) heavy cream

Sugared Cranberries (page 16), for garnish, optional

Sliced oranges, for garnish, optional

UPPING *the* PIE GAME

"Food is about making an interaction with ingredients. If you talk to them, they will always tell you a story."

Josè Andrès

Growing up, I was never a fan of pies and tarts. It wasn't until I was an exchange student in Switzerland and would visit France on the weekends that I really began to appreciate the intricacy of seasonal fruits and everyday pantry ingredients. Fresh, sun-ripened, local fruit combined with a delicious buttery tart shell was pretty much a life-changing discovery for me! Since then, pies and tarts have been two of my favorite, all-occasion desserts to make and serve.

ROASTED GRAPE TART

This recipe is an ode to my heritage. To the days spent making hundreds of pounds of Italian cookies with my Sicilian grandfather during the holidays. To the Sunday mornings that we would wake up to the smell of onions and garlic caramelizing for the perfect, still impossible to replicate, tomato pasta sauce. If he were still around, I'm sure he would be proud of this Italiano tart.

MAKES: 10 to 12 servings

To roast the grapes, preheat the oven to 425°F (218°C). Line an 18 x 13-inch (46 x 33-cm) baking dish with foil or parchment paper. Scatter the grape halves on the pan.

In a medium-sized bowl, combine the oil, vinegar, water, vanilla bean paste and honey. Whisk them together until combined, then pour it over the grape halves. Roast the grapes for 25 minutes or until they begin to pop. Remove them from the oven and cool them completely. Reduce the oven heat to 350°F (177°C).

To make the amaretti crust, in a medium-sized bowl, toss the amaretti crumbs and salt with melted butter until the mixture is moistened. Press the crumbs evenly over the bottom and halfway up the sides of a fluted rectangle or 9-inch (23-cm) round springform tart pan. Bake at 350°F (177°C) for 10 minutes, or until the crust is set. Cool it completely on a wire rack before adding the mascarpone filling.

To make the filling, in a small bowl, combine the mascarpone, sugar, lemon juice and vanilla and beat until smooth. Spread the mixture evenly in the cooled tart shell. Top it with the roasted grapes and chopped pistachios. Chill it until you're ready to serve. Right before serving, drizzle the tart with extra honey and sprinkle it with a bit of flaked sea salt.

BAKER'S NOTES ~

If amaretti cookies are unavailable, make a graham cracker crust (page 85) and add ¼ teaspoon of almond extract to the crust mixture before pulsing.

When picking grapes, look for grapes that are firmly attached to their stem. If picking dark grapes, make sure they are dark and rich in color.

ROASTED GRAPES

12 oz (340 g) black seedless grapes, halved

1 tbsp (15 ml) extra virgin olive oil

1 tsp balsamic vinegar

2 tsp (10 ml) water

2 tsp (14 g) vanilla bean paste, or vanilla extract

2 tsp (10 ml) honey, plus more for garnish

AMARETTI CRUST

2 cups (170 g) finely crushed amaretti cookies

¼ tsp salt

7 tbsp (105 ml) unsalted butter, melted

MASCARPONE FILLING

2 cups (460 g) mascarpone cheese, room temperature

¼ cup (33 g) powdered sugar

1 tsp fresh lemon juice

1 tsp vanilla extract

¼ cup (25 g) pistachios, chopped, for garnish

Flaked sea salt, for garnish

CHOCOLATE-POMEGRANATE TART

So many fruits pair well with chocolate, but pomegranate is one of my favorites. The tartness of the arils complements the dark chocolate so well, and they add a gorgeous burst of contrasting color. Pomegranate arils make the perfect garnish for desserts, especially this one.

MAKES: 8 to 10 servings

To make the crust, in a food processor, pulse the flour, cocoa powder, sugar and salt until they're combined. Add the chilled butter and pulse until the mixture becomes crumbly. Add the egg yolks, cream and vanilla and pulse until the dough is no longer dry and begins forming large clumps. If you're not using a food processor, use a pastry cutter or fork to cut the butter into the dry crust ingredients. Add the remaining wet ingredients and combine them until the mixture forms a ball.

Preheat the oven to 350°F (177°C). Evenly press the dough into a 9-inch (23-cm) tart pan and pierce the bottom a few times with a fork. Cover it with foil and freeze it for 15 minutes.

Place the foil-covered tart in the oven to bake for 20 to 22 minutes. Remove the foil and bake for 5 minutes. Remove the crust from the oven and cool it on a wire rack for 30 minutes.

To make the filling, in a medium-sized heat-proof bowl, place the butter and chopped chocolate. Heat the heavy cream in a microwave-safe dish for 1 minute. Once hot, pour the cream over the bowl of butter and chocolate chips. Allow the chocolate to rest for 5 minutes, then stir until it's smooth. If there are still clumps of chocolate, return the bowl to the microwave and heat it for 10-second increments, stirring after every time, until it's smooth. Stir in the pomegranate juice and ½ cup (88 g) of the pomegranate arils. Pour the filling into the crust and let it sit. After about 10 minutes, sprinkle the remaining arils over the top of the tart. Continue to let the tart sit at room temperature until the ganache has set, about 3 hours, or refrigerate it for 1 hour.

When you're ready to serve, run a knife under hot water, then wipe it dry. Slice the tart and serve it with a dollop of whipped cream, if desired.

CRUST

1½ cups (180 g) all-purpose flour

¼ cup (30 g) dark cocoa powder

½ cup (100 g) granulated sugar

½ tsp salt

½ cup (120 g) unsalted butter, chilled and sliced

2 large egg yolks

3 tbsp (45 ml) heavy cream

1 tsp vanilla extract

FILLING

3 tbsp (40 g) butter

1¼ cups (230 g) dark chocolate, cut into small pieces

1¼ cups (300 ml) heavy cream

2 tbsp (30 ml) pomegranate juice

1 cup (175 g) pomegranate arils, divided

Whipped cream, for serving, optional

BAKER'S NOTE ~

Add a bit of orange zest and flaked sea salt to the top of your tart to add a bit more color and flavor.

FALL'S BEST APPLE-PEAR PIE

Every year at the beginning of September, we take our kids to a quaint little town about an hour away. The streets of Julian are peppered with antique stores and the best pie shops on the West Coast. After spending the day shopping, eating and apple and pear picking, the kids and I come home and bake a fresh homemade pie. It is one of our favorite days of the year, and hopefully one that they will always remember. This pie encompasses the sweet, crisp, tart flavors of fall with cinnamon and nutmeg–sprinkled apples and pears.

MAKES: 10 servings

To make the buttermilk crusts, in a large bowl, combine the flour, sugar and salt. Using a pastry cutter, cut the butter and shortening into the flour until the mixture resembles a coarse meal. Stir in the cold buttermilk until large clumps form.

If you're making it in a food processor, pulse together the flour, sugar and salt. Add the cold butter and shortening and pulse just until the mixture is crumbly. While pulsing, add the buttermilk. Pulse until the mixture is moist and clumps form. Do not overprocess.

Press the dough together to form two balls. Shape each ball into a disk in between two pieces of wax paper. Refrigerate them for 1 hour.

To make the filling, in a large bowl, toss the pears, apples, sugar, lemon juice, cinnamon and nutmeg together.

Preheat the oven to 350°F (177°C).

To assemble the pie, roll out one disc of dough into an 11- or 12-inch (28- or 30-cm) circle on a lightly floured surface. Alternatively, roll the dough directly inbetween wax paper layers. Line the bottom of a 9-inch (23-cm) pie pan and trim it so it lays about ½ inch (1.3 cm) over the edge of the pan. Fill it with the apple-pear filling and dollop it with butter. Roll out the remaining dough into an 11- or 12-inch (28- or 30-cm) circle. Top the filling with the top crust and trim the edges to the same overhang as the bottom crust. Cover and refrigerate the excess crust dough. Fold the top layer of dough under the edge of the bottom layer and press the edges together to seal, then crimp the edges or press them with a fork. Roll out the remaining excess dough and cut it with a leaf cookie cutter. Decorate the top crust with the dough leaves.

Brush the surface of the dough with the beaten egg and then sprinkle it with sugar and cinnamon. Cover the pie loosely with foil. Bake the pie for 30 minutes, then remove the foil and bake for 30 to 35 minutes or until the crust is golden brown and crisp. Serve it warm or at room temperature.

BUTTERMILK PIE CRUST

2½ cups (300 g) all-purpose flour

2 tbsp (25 g) granulated sugar

1 tsp salt

½ cup (120 g) unsalted butter, cold

½ cup (100 g) solid vegetable shortening or lard, chilled

½ cup (120 ml) cold full-fat buttermilk

APPLE-PEAR FILLING

3 medium ripe pears, peeled, cored and thinly sliced

3 medium tart apples, peeled, cored and thinly sliced

1 cup (200 g) granulated sugar

1 tsp lemon juice

1 tsp ground cinnamon

¼ tsp ground nutmeg

3 tbsp (40 g) butter

1 egg, slightly beaten

1 tsp granulated sugar

¼ tsp cinnamon

BANANA CRÈME BRÛLÉE TART *with* HAZELNUT CRUST

Now, with this tart, you can enjoy two delectable desserts in one! The hazelnut crust with banana cream filling is topped off with a perfectly burnt sugar coating. Careful though—you probably won't want to share!

MAKES: 8 to 10 servings

To make the crust, using an electric mixer, cream the butter and powdered sugar until it's smooth. Add the egg and mix until incorporated. Add the flour, ground hazelnuts and salt and mix until it's just combined. Using your hands or the bottom of a lightly floured measuring cup, evenly press the dough into a 9-inch (23-cm) tart shell with a removable bottom. Chill the crust for 1 hour.

Preheat the oven to 350°F (177°F). Line the inside of the chilled crust with foil. Fill the foil with pie weights, uncooked rice or dried beans. Bake the crust (with pie weights) for 15 minutes. Carefully remove the foil and weights and return the tart to the oven to cook for 5 minutes. Set it aside to cool while you're making the filling.

To make the custard filling, in a large saucepan, heat the heavy cream, vanilla bean pod and seeds and salt over medium-low heat. Bring it to a simmer, then remove it from the heat.

In a separate bowl, whisk the egg yolks and brown sugar until it's light and smooth. Whisk in the pureed banana. Remove the vanilla bean pod from the cream. Gradually add 1 cup (240 ml) of the hot cream to the egg yolk mixture, whisking constantly to combine. Pour the egg mixture into the cream, and return the pot to medium-low heat. Continue stirring the mixture until it coats the back of the spoon. Stir in the softened butter. Carefully pour the banana custard into the hazelnut crust and spread it evenly. Let the tart sit at room temperature until cool, then refrigerate it for 2 to 3 hours.

When you're ready to serve, garnish it with the sliced banana and sprinkle the entire custard surface with 4 tablespoons (50 g) of sugar. Holding the kitchen torch at least 6 inches (15 cm) from the tart, carefully caramelize the sugar and the sugar-coated bananas. Slice and serve it immediately.

BAKER'S NOTE ～

If you don't have a kitchen torch, place the tart under the broiler for about two minutes. Don't leave it unattended, as it will quickly burn.

CRUST

1¼ cups (290 g) unsalted butter, softened

¾ cup (90 g) powdered sugar

1 large egg

1½ cups (180 g) all-purpose flour

⅓ cup (25 g) hazelnuts, peeled, toasted, finely ground

¼ tsp salt

CUSTARD FILLING

2 cups (480 ml) heavy cream

1 vanilla bean pod, split, seeds set aside

¼ tsp salt

4 large egg yolks

¾ cup (170 g) light brown sugar, firmly packed

½ cup (120 ml) banana puree, 1-2 ripe bananas

4 tbsp (60 g) unsalted butter, softened

TOPPING

1 banana, sliced

4 tbsp (50 g) granulated sugar

RASPBERRY-RICOTTA CHEESECAKE

I once made this dessert and posted it on Instagram. Within a few minutes, I had a private message from Williams-Sonoma asking to repost the image. That was a good day. Needless to say, this studded raspberry cheesecake is beautiful and quite the showstopper. If you are not yet convinced of the natural beauty of fruit and how well it can decorate the dish, then here is your proof!

MAKES: 8 to 10 servings

Preheat the oven to 350°F (177°C).

To make the crust, in a medium-sized bowl, mix together the ground graham crackers, sugar, melted butter and salt until the crumbs are evenly moistened. Using your hands, evenly press it into a 9-inch (23-cm) fluted tart pan with a removable base. Set it aside.

To make the filling, in a medium-sized bowl, beat the ricotta, cream cheese, lemon zest and lemon juice until it's light and smooth, about 3 minutes. Add the sugar, flour and salt and continue beating until it's well combined. Add the egg yolks and beat until it's just combined. Pour the filling into the crust and spread it evenly.

Bake the tart for 30 to 35 minutes or until the edges are set but the center jiggles slightly when moved. Let the cheesecake cool completely, then refrigerate it for 2 to 3 hours. Right before serving, garnish it with fresh raspberries and a dusting of powdered sugar.

BAKER'S NOTE ~

For an extra raspberry punch, stir a few berries into the cheesecake mixture before baking.

CRUST

1 cup (90 g) graham crackers, finely ground, about 8 whole graham crackers

2 tbsp (25 g) granulated sugar

4 tbsp (60 ml) unsalted butter, melted

½ tsp salt

FILLING

1½ cups (190 g) whole-milk ricotta

½ cup (115 g) cream cheese, room temperature

1 tbsp (10 g) lemon zest, finely grated

1 tbsp (15 ml) lemon juice

¾ cup (150 g) granulated sugar

2 tbsp (15 g) all-purpose flour

¼ tsp salt

3 large egg yolks

9 oz (255 g) fresh raspberries, washed and dried, for garnish

Powdered sugar for dusting

PEACH BAKEWELL TART

Prior to watching The Great British Baking Show, *I had never heard of a Bakewell tart. Since then, I make them all the time. While not traditional, I love adding fresh fruit to the almond filling, especially peaches.*

MAKES: 8 to 10 servings

To make the *pâte sucrée*, in a large bowl, whisk together the flour, sugar and salt. Rub in the butter using your fingertips until the mixture resembles fine breadcrumbs. Using a mixer, beat the egg yolk, heavy cream and vanilla into the flour mixture on low speed until it's just combined. Turn out the dough onto a lightly floured surface and roll it out to a ¼-inch (0.6-cm)-thick round. Press the dough into a 9-inch (23-cm)-deep fluted tart pan with a removable bottom and refrigerate it for 30 minutes.

Preheat the oven to 350°F (177°C).

For the fruit filling, once the crust has chilled, spread the peach jam over the base of the crust and arrange the sliced peaches over the jam.

To make the frangipane filling, in a medium-sized bowl, cream the butter and sugar together until it's pale and light. Add the almond flour, egg and almond extract and mix them together until smooth. Spoon the frangipane mixture over the peaches, spreading it evenly to cover them.

Place the tart pan on a baking sheet and bake for 45 to 50 minutes or until the crust is crisp and the tart is golden brown. Once done, place the tart pan on a cooling rack and cool it for 30 minutes.

Right before serving, make the glacé. Heat the jam in a microwave-safe dish for 20 seconds. Whisk the powdered sugar into the melted jam. If needed, add a teaspoon of water to the mixture until your icing has a smooth and thick pouring consistency. Zigzag the icing with a spoon over the tart. Garnish it with a few slivered almonds, if desired.

BAKER'S NOTE ~

These can also be made into five to six cute individual tarts. Adjust the baking time to 30 to 32 minutes.

PÂTÉ SUCRÉE

1 cup (120 g) all-purpose flour

¼ cup (50 g) granulated sugar

⅛ tsp salt

4 tbsp (60 g) cold unsalted butter, cut into pieces

1 large egg yolk

1 tsp heavy cream

¼ tsp vanilla extract

FRUIT FILLING

4 tbsp (80 g) peach jam or jelly

2 fresh peaches, peeled and sliced

FRANGIPANE FILLING

12 tbsp (180 g) unsalted butter, softened

¾ cup (150 g) granulated sugar

1½ cups (150 g) almond flour

1 large egg, slightly beaten

1 tsp almond extract

GLACÉ

2 tbsp (40 g) peach jam or jelly

1 cup (120 g) powdered sugar

1 tsp water, if needed

½ cup (55 g) slivered almonds, for garnish, optional

NECTARINE GALETTE

Nectarines don't get nearly as much attention as peaches, and I never understood why. With similar flavors, they are much easier to cook with because you do not have to peel them. They are excellent in pies, tarts or any dessert. Sometimes I wish that we could make all pies in the form of this simple rustic galette. This free-form pie has so much character and lets the fruit really shine.

MAKES: 6 to 8 servings

To make the pie crust, in a large bowl, whisk together the flour, salt and sugar. Using your hands or a pastry cutter, cut the butter into the flour mixture until the mixture resembles a crumbly, sandy mixture. Drizzle the water and vinegar over the mixture and knead until the dough begins to form a ball. Alternatively, make the dough using a food processor using the same steps above, but only processing the dough just enough to come together. Shape the dough into a round, flat disk and wrap it tightly with plastic wrap. Refrigerate it for 1 hour. Or refrigerate it for up to 48 hours or freeze it up to 1 month, allowing the dough to stand at room temperature for 30 minutes just before using it.

Once the dough is chilled, preheat the oven to 375°F (191°C). Line a baking sheet with parchment paper.

To make the filling, add the nectarine slices to a large bowl. Cover the slices with the flour, granulated sugar, cinnamon and salt. Toss the nectarines until each slice is coated with the flour mixture. Set it aside.

On a lightly floured surface, roll out the dough into a circle about ¼ inch (0.6 cm) thick. Transfer the circle to the parchment-lined baking sheet.

To assemble it, decoratively arrange the nectarine slices on top of the dough in concentric circles or in slightly overlapping rows, leaving a 2-inch (5-cm) border around the perimeter of the dough. Fold the pastry edge up and over the nectarines to create a 1-inch (2.5-cm) border.

In a small bowl, whisk together the egg and milk. Using a pastry brush, brush the edges of the galette with the egg wash, then sprinkle the entire galette with the sugar.

Bake for 40 to 45 minutes or until the juices are bubbling and the crust is golden brown. Cool it for 20 minutes before serving. Serve it warm or at room temperature.

CRUST

2¼ cups (270 g) all-purpose flour

1 tsp salt

1 tsp granulated sugar

12 tbsp (180 g) cold unsalted butter, cut into pieces

¼ cup (60 ml) ice-cold water; strain the ice cubes just before using

1 tsp white vinegar

FILLING

6 cups (860 g) nectarines, washed, sliced

3 tbsp (25 g) all-purpose flour

⅓ cup (70 g) granulated sugar

2 tsp (5 g) ground cinnamon

⅛ tsp salt

1 large egg

2 tsp (10 ml) milk

2 tsp (8 g) granulated sugar

BERRY FRIED HAND PIES

Every year my kids get a choice: either they get to go to the county fair, or I give them half of the money I would have spent at the fair and make them their favorite food. Without fail, they choose the latter. So in July of every year, we spend the day making these pies and going shopping. I think it's a pretty good trade-off.

MAKES: 16 hand pies

To make the crust, in a large bowl or your food processor, combine the flour, sugar and salt. Cut the butter slices into the flour using a pastry cutter or pulse it in a food processor until it forms small pea-sized clumps. Add the ice water and mix until the dough forms a large ball. Separate the dough into two disks. Wrap the disks in plastic wrap and refrigerate them for at least an hour.

To make the filling, in a medium-sized saucepan, stir together the berries, cornstarch, sugar, salt and lemon juice over medium-high heat. Bring the mixture to a simmer, stirring regularly, then reduce the heat to low and cook until the mixture begins to thicken, about 5 minutes. Pour the mixture into a bowl and set it aside to cool completely. The berry filling can be made a day ahead and stored in an airtight container in the refrigerator.

In a small bowl, whisk together the egg and water with a fork.

On a clean, floured surface, roll out the chilled dough to a ⅓-inch (0.8-cm)-thick rectangle. Cut the dough into eight even squares. Lay the pastry squares on a parchment paper–lined baking sheet. Dollop a heaping teaspoon of the berry filling into the bottom right corner of each square. Lightly brush the edges of the square with the egg wash. Fold the top left corner of the square over the filling to the bottom right corner and gently press the edges together. Pinch the edges together to create a ripple, or create a fluted seal by gently pressing the edges down with the back of a fork. Place the first batch of hand pies in the refrigerator to chill while making the next batch with the remaining dough.

To fry the pies, heat approximately 2½ inches (6 cm) of vegetable oil in a medium-sized saucepan over medium-high heat. Fit a deep-fry thermometer to the edge of the pan and heat the oil to 360°F (182°C). Line a large baking sheet with a metal baking rack and set it aside. In a small bowl, whisk together the cinnamon and sugar topping and set it aside. Working in batches of two pies, gently place the hand pies into the hot oil. Fry the pies until they're golden brown on both sides, about 4 minutes, flipping once in between. Remove the pies from the oil and place them on the prepared baking sheet. Immediately sprinkle them with 1 teaspoon of the cinnamon-sugar topping. Repeat with the remaining pies.

CRUST

2½ cups (300 g) all-purpose flour, plus more for rolling

1½ tbsp (20 g) granulated sugar

½ tsp of salt

1 cup (230 g) cold unsalted butter, cut into slices

⅔ cup (160 ml) ice water

BERRY FILLING

2 cups (250 g) assorted fresh berries, washed and dried

2 tbsp (20 g) cornstarch

⅓ cup (70 g) sugar

⅛ tsp salt

1 tbsp (15 ml) fresh lemon juice

1 large egg

2 tsp (10 ml) water

Vegetable oil, for frying

TOPPING

1 tsp cinnamon

¼ cup (50 g) granulated sugar

CLASSIC FRENCH FRUIT TART

This French staple is displayed in every bakery and grocery store in France and Switzerland, and rightfully so because it is so beautiful. After a few years of resisting the urge to dip my feet into French pastries due to feeling intimidated, I finally did. Here's the thing with French recipes—they are not really difficult as much as they are time consuming. But when you are thoroughly enjoying the fruits of your labor, does it even matter how long it took to make?

MAKES: 10 servings

To make the *pâté sucrée*, in a large bowl, whisk together the flour, sugar and salt. Using your fingertips, rub in the butter until the mixture resembles fine breadcrumbs. Using a mixer, beat the egg yolk, heavy cream and vanilla with the flour mixture on low speed until they're just combined. Turn out the dough onto a lightly floured surface and roll it out to ¼-inch (0.6-cm) thickness. Transfer the dough to a 9-inch (23-cm)-deep fluted tart pan with removable bottom and refrigerate it for 30 minutes.

Preheat the oven to 375°F (191°C). Line the inside of the chilled pâté sucrée with foil or parchment paper. Fill the foil or parchment with pie weights or dried beans up to the edges. Bake for 25 to 27 minutes or until the crust begins to look dry. Carefully remove the foil and weights and bake for 10 to 15 minutes, or until the crust is a light golden brown. Remove the tart from the oven, and cool it completely before filling it.

Bring a cup (240 ml) of water to a simmer in the bottom of a double boiler. Place the chocolate in a large bowl, and then set it over the pan of steaming water. Stir the chocolate until it's melted and smooth. Alternatively, melt the chocolate in the microwave in a microwave-safe dish for 30 seconds on high. Carefully pour the melted chocolate into the cooled crust and spread it evenly using an offset spatula or the back of a spoon. Chill the tart while making the pastry cream.

(continued)

PÂTÉ SUCRÉE

1 cup (120 g) all-purpose flour

¼ cup (50 g) granulated sugar

⅛ tsp salt

4 tbsp (60 g) unsalted butter, cold, cut into pieces

1 large egg yolk

1 tsp heavy cream

¼ tsp vanilla extract

1½ oz (43 g) white or semisweet chocolate, finely chopped

To make the pastry cream, in a heavy-bottomed saucepan, heat the milk, cream, vanilla bean pod plus seeds and salt over medium heat. Bring the mixture to a simmer, then remove it from the heat.

In a separate bowl, whisk the egg yolks, sugar and cornstarch together until it's light and pale. Remove the vanilla bean pod from the cream. Temper the eggs by gradually adding 1 cup (240 ml) of the hot cream to the egg yolk mixture, whisking constantly to combine them. Pour the egg mixture back into the cream, and return the pot to medium-low heat. Continue stirring the mixture until it begins to thicken and coats the back of the spoon. Stir in the softened butter. Pour the pastry cream into the tart shell and refrigerate until it's cold and firm, about 3 hours.

To serve, garnish the tart with the kiwis, strawberries, oranges, blueberries and raspberries. Heat the apricot preserves in a microwave-safe dish for 20 seconds, or until it's melted and runny. Using a pastry brush, brush the fruit with the preserves. Slice and serve.

BAKER'S NOTE ～

While this tart is best served the same day, you can prepare the tart shell and custard up to one day in advance. The white chocolate layer acts as a barrier between the pastry cream and the tart shell and avoids a soggy crust. Garnish it with fruits the same day as serving.

VANILLA BEAN PASTRY CREAM

1½ cups (360 ml) whole milk

½ cup (120 ml) heavy cream

1 vanilla bean pod, sliced in half and seeds scraped

⅛ tsp salt

5 large egg yolks

½ cup (100 g) granulated sugar

3 tbsp (30 g) cornstarch

4 tbsp (60 g) unsalted butter, softened

FRUIT TOPPING

3–4 kiwis, peeled and sliced evenly

10–12 strawberries, hulled and sliced in half

¼ cup (50 g) mandarin oranges, drained

½ cup (50 g) fresh blueberries

¼ cup (35 g) fresh raspberries

¼ cup (80 g) apricot preserves, warmed

MILE-HIGH LEMON MERINGUE PIE

When I cook, I use the motto "Go Big or Go Home," especially when it comes to this pie. I always have an abundance of lemons that need to be used, so making a deep-dish, deliciously tart lemon filling is a must. And with a big bottom, you have to have a big top, right?!

MAKES: 10 servings

To make the pie crust, in a medium-sized bowl, whisk together the flour, salt and sugar. Using your hands or a pastry cutter, cut the butter into the flour mixture until the mixture resembles a crumbly, sandy mixture. Drizzle the water and vinegar over the mixture and knead until the dough begins to form a ball. Alternatively, make the dough in a food processor using the same steps above, only processing the dough just enough to come together. Shape the dough into a round, flat disk and wrap it tightly with plastic wrap. Refrigerate it for 1 hour. Or refrigerate it for up to 48 hours or freeze it up to 1 month, allowing the dough to stand at room temperature for 30 minutes just before using it.

Preheat the oven to 375°F (191°C). Once the dough is cold, roll it out into a ¼-inch (0.6-cm)-thick circle on a lightly floured surface. Transfer the dough to a 9-inch (23-cm) deep-dish pie plate. Trim the pastry to ½ inch (1.3 cm) beyond the rim of the plate, then flute or crimp the edges. Line the inside of the crust with foil or parchment paper. Fill the foil all the way up using pie weights, uncooked rice or dried beans. Bake for 25 to 27 minutes, or until the edges are beginning to turn golden. Remove the pie from the oven, then carefully grasp the corners of the foil and lift it to remove the pie weights. Return the crust to the oven and cook for 10 to 15 minutes or until the bottom of the crust looks dry and is lightly golden. Remove it from the oven and cool it completely.

(continued)

PERFECT PIE CRUST

1½ cups (180 g) all-purpose flour

½ tsp salt

½ tsp granulated sugar

6 tbsp (80 g) cold unsalted butter, cut into pieces

3 tbsp (45 ml) ice water; strain the ice cubes just before using

½ tsp white vinegar

To make the lemon filling, in a medium-sized saucepan, whisk together the sugar, flour, cornstarch and salt. Add the egg yolks and whisk until the mixture is a pale-yellow color. Whisk in the lemon juice. Place the pan over medium-high heat and bring it to a light boil. Remove it from the heat and stir in 3 tablespoons (40 g) of the butter. Pour the lemon filling into the prebaked pie crust. Carefully rub the remaining tablespoon (15 g) of butter over the lemon filling to avoid forming a skin on the filling. Refrigerate the pie until it's cold, about 3 hours.

When the pie is chilled, make the meringue topping. Preheat the oven to 350°F (177°C). In a large, clean metal bowl, beat the egg whites on medium until frothy. Add the sugar and increase the beater speed to high. Beat until stiff peaks form. Spread the meringue over the lemon filling and slightly over the edges of the crust to ensure that the filling is sealed. Bake the pie for 10 to 15 minutes or until the meringue has turned a golden-brown color. Remove it from the oven and cool it on a wire rack. Once cooled, loosely cover the pie and store it in the refrigerator for up to 3 days.

BAKER'S NOTE ~

Use a store-bought pie crust to replace the homemade version if you're short on time.

LEMON FILLING

1½ cups (300 g) granulated sugar

3 tbsp (25 g) all-purpose flour

¼ cup (40 g) cornstarch

⅓ tsp salt

6 large egg yolks

1½ cups (360 ml) fresh lemon juice

4 tbsp (60 g) unsalted butter, divided

MERINGUE TOPPING

6 egg whites

½ cup (100 g) granulated sugar

PALOMA TART

Inspired by one of my favorite cocktails, this tart features a luscious grapefruit curd with a touch of tequila in a buttery lime and coconut crust and topped with a lime-infused whipped cream.

MAKES: 8 to 10 servings

Preheat the oven to 350°F (177°C). Lightly spray a 9-inch (23-cm) fluted tart pan with nonstick cooking spray.

To make the crust, in a large bowl, mix the powdered sugar, flour, salt, lime zest and coconut until they're well blended, about 30 seconds. Add the butter and lime juice; mix to combine them until moist clumps form. Press the dough into the bottom and up the sides of the pan. Bake the crust until it's golden brown, about 23 to 25 minutes. Cool it for 10 minutes.

While the crust is cooling, make the curd. In a heavy-bottomed, medium-sized pot, whisk the egg yolks and sugar until it's light and pale. Whisk in the salt, grapefruit zest, juice and cornstarch. Place the pot on the stove over medium heat and cook the curd until it thickens and coats the back of a spoon, about 5 minutes. Remove it from the heat; stir in the butter, one tablespoon (15 g) at a time, and then add the tequila, if using.

Pour the warm curd into the crust; let it sit for 30 minutes, then transfer the tart to the refrigerator to chill for at least 1 hour.

Right before serving, make the whipped cream. Beat the heavy whipping cream, powdered sugar and lime zest on high until stiff peaks form. Dollop the cream onto the tart and garnish it with lime and grapefruit wedges.

BAKER'S NOTE ⁓

When making the curd, it is necessary to whisk the egg yolks and sugar before adding the citrus juice to avoiding curdling.

CRUST

½ cup (65 g) powdered sugar

2 cups (240 g) all-purpose flour

¼ tsp salt

1 tbsp (10 g) lime zest, freshly grated

½ cup (40 g) coconut, shredded

1 cup (230 g) unsalted butter, cold

1 tbsp (15 ml) fresh lime juice

GRAPEFRUIT TEQUILA CURD

6 egg yolks

1¼ cups (300 g) granulated sugar

¼ tsp salt

1 tbsp (10 g) grapefruit zest

2 cups (480 ml) grapefruit juice, freshly squeezed

¼ cup (40 g) cornstarch

3 tbsp (40 g) unsalted butter, cold

1 tbsp (15 ml) tequila, optional

WHIPPED CREAM

1½ cups (360 ml) heavy whipping cream, cold

1½ tbsp (12 g) powdered sugar

½ tbsp (5 g) lime zest, freshly grated

Lime and grapefruit wedges, for garnish

FORKS *Not* REQUIRED

"Pull up a chair, take a taste. Come join us. Life is so endlessly delicious."

— Ruth Reichl

I've been told I'm fearless, maybe even reckless . . . in the kitchen. I'm passionate about experimenting with flavor and unexpected ingredients. When getting my guinea pigs, a.k.a. family members, to taste-test my creations, I often think of this quote: St. Augustine is said to have uttered the words, "The world is a book and those who do not travel, read only one page." It's kind of the same thing with the classic chocolate chip cookie! If you haven't branched out yet, it's time to take your taste buds on a culinary voyage. Swap out those boring chocolate chips for fresh blueberries and white chocolate and take that cookie to a whole new level. This chapter will provide you with the best recipes that meld together common desserts and fruit masterpieces into one handheld delicacy. Just as you would bite into a fresh, juicy peach, you can take a bite out of these—no fork required!

BLACKBERRY CUSTARD BARS

These custard bars combine two of my favorite things: a deliciously sweet custard and a buttery crust. Add in the sun-ripened sweet berries, and it's perfect. These bars are perfect for an afternoon picnic with friends and a crisp glass of white wine.

MAKES: 9 to 12 servings

Preheat the oven to 350°F (177°C). Line a 9 x 13-inch (23 x 33-cm) baking dish with parchment paper.

For the crust, in a medium-sized bowl, mix together the flour, sugar and salt. Pour in the melted butter and mix with a fork until small pea-sized lumps form. Press the crust dough into the bottom and sides of the baking dish. Bake for 10 minutes or until the sides of the shortbread turn golden brown. Remove it from the oven and cool it for 10 minutes.

To make the custard, use a blender or an electric mixer and blend the melted butter, milk and eggs until combined. Add the sugar, flour, salt and vanilla and mix or blend them until completely smooth. Scatter the berries over the slightly cooled crust. Pour the custard batter over the berries.

Bake until the custard is set, about 32 to 35 minutes. Cool it completely, then refrigerate it for 1 hour before cutting it. Slice it into 9 to 12 squares. Sift the powdered sugar on top right before serving.

BAKER'S NOTE ～

These custard bars can be made with any berry or combination of berries.

CRUST

2 cups (240 g) all-purpose flour

½ cup (100 g) granulated sugar

¼ tsp salt

1 cup (240 ml) unsalted butter, melted

CUSTARD

½ cup (120 ml) unsalted butter, melted

1½ cups (360 ml) whole milk

6 large eggs

¾ cup (150 g) granulated sugar

1 cup (120 g) all-purpose flour

½ tsp salt

1 tsp pure vanilla extract

2 cups (290 g) blackberries

¼ cup (35 g) sifted powdered sugar, for garnish

LEMON CHEESECAKE BARS

I always have a dilemma when standing in front of a dessert bar. Do I go for the cheesecake or the lemon bars? This question had me thinking. Why do we have to make these kinds of decisions when the two pair so beautifully together? With that, these delicious bars were born.

MAKES: 9 to 12 servings

Preheat the oven to 350°F (177°C). Line an 8 x 8-inch (20 x 20-cm) baking dish with parchment paper or spray it with nonstick cooking spray.

To make the crust, in a medium-sized bowl, beat the butter and sugar together for at least 5 minutes, or until it's light and fluffy. Beat in the flour and salt until they're combined. The dough will be crumbly. Press it evenly into the bottom of the prepared pan. Bake the crust for 15 minutes. When done, remove the pan from the oven and set it aside to cool before adding the remaining layers. Reduce the oven temperature to 325°F (163°C).

To make the lemon layer, in a small bowl, whisk together the eggs, sugar, flour, lemon zest and lemon juice until it's smooth. Pour the lemon mixture over the shortbread crust.

To make the cheesecake layer, in a separate bowl, beat the softened cream cheese and sugar together until it's smooth. Beat in the egg, vanilla, lemon juice and zest until they're combined.

Spread the cheesecake filling over the lemon mixture. The layers will separate during baking.

Bake for 25 to 28 minutes, or until the filling is set. Remove it from the oven and cool it to room temperature, then refrigerate until it's cold, about 1 hour.

To make the sour cream layer, in a small bowl, whisk the sour cream and powdered sugar until it's smooth. Spread it over the cheesecake and refrigerate it for 30 minutes. Garnish the bar with fresh berries, if desired. Cut into 9 or 12 squares.

SHORTBREAD CRUST

½ cup (120 g) unsalted butter, room temperature

½ cup (100 g) granulated sugar

1 cup (120 g) all-purpose flour

¼ tsp salt

LEMON LAYER

2 large eggs

¾ cup (150 g) granulated sugar

½ tbsp (4 g) all-purpose flour

1 tbsp (10 g) lemon zest

¼ cup (60 ml) lemon juice

CHEESECAKE LAYER

1 (8-oz [227-g]) package cream cheese, room temperature

⅓ cup (70 g) granulated sugar

1 large egg

1 tsp vanilla extract

1 tbsp (15 ml) lemon juice

½ tsp lemon zest

SOUR CREAM LAYER

¾ cup (170 g) sour cream

1 tbsp (8 g) powdered sugar

Fresh berries, for garnish, optional

BOURBON-CHERRY BROWN BUTTER BARS

Bourbon, cherries and brown butter are like a match made in dessert heaven. Serve this bar with a small glass of good-quality bourbon on the rocks, and the cherries and brown butter will accentuate the smooth and rich cherry and oak tasting notes of the liquor. This is one of those recipes that makes you sound like you really know what you are talking about and that you are a bourbon connoisseur, even if you haven't a clue. It's a millennial thing.

MAKES: 9 to 12 servings

Preheat the oven to 350°F (177°C). Line an 8 x 8-inch (20 x 20-cm) baking dish with parchment paper or spray it with nonstick cooking spray.

To make the crust, in a medium-sized bowl, beat the butter and sugar together for at least 5 minutes, or until it's light and fluffy. Mix in the flour and salt until they're combined. The dough will be crumbly. Press it evenly into the bottom of the prepared pan. Bake the crust for 15 minutes. Remove the pan from the oven and set it aside to cool before adding the filling.

To make the brown butter, add the cubed butter to a small saucepan over medium heat for 4 to 5 minutes. Watch carefully as the butter melts, stirring occasionally until the butter turns an amber color and begins to smell nutty. Set it aside to cool for 5 minutes before making the filling.

To make the filling, in a medium-sized bowl, whisk together the sugar, eggs, salt, flour, vanilla, brown butter and bourbon, if using, until it's smooth. Pour it over the crust and top that with the cherry halves. Bake for 35 to 40 minutes, or until the filling is golden brown and set. Cool it completely before cutting it into 9 or 12 squares.

BAKER'S NOTE

If you're making a non-alcoholic version, omit the bourbon and decrease the flour to ¼ cup (30 g).

SHORTBREAD CRUST

½ cup (120 g) unsalted butter, room temperature

½ cup (100 g) granulated sugar

1 cup (120 g) all-purpose flour

¼ tsp salt

FILLING

½ cup (120 g) unsalted butter, cubed

½ cup (100 g) granulated sugar

2 large eggs

¼ tsp salt

⅓ cup (45 g) all-purpose flour

1 tsp vanilla extract

1 tbsp (15 ml) bourbon, optional

1 cup (230 g) cherries, pitted and cut in half

APRICOT-OATMEAL BARS

If you are looking for a dessert that travels well and is perfect for a snack or a picnic, these bars are it. They are as if an oatmeal cookie and coffee cake made an apricot-infused baby. I wish re-creating humans was that easy.

MAKES: 9 to 12 servings

To make the filling, in a small saucepan, bring the apricots, sugar, lemon juice and cornstarch to a simmer over medium heat. Cook for 10 to 15 minutes or until the apricots have begun to break down and the juice has thickened. Remove it from the heat and cool it to room temperature.

Preheat the oven to 350°F (177°C). Line an 8 x 8-inch (20 x 20-cm) baking dish with parchment paper.

To make the crust, in a large bowl, whisk together the flour, oats, brown sugar, baking soda, cinnamon and salt. Add the butter and combine them with your hands or a fork until the mixture is crumbly. Press three-fourths of the mixture into the bottom of the lined pan. Spread the apricot filling on top of the bottom layer, and then sprinkle it with the remaining flour/oat mixture.

Bake for 30 to 35 minutes or until the mixture is golden brown. Cool it completely before slicing it into 9 or 12 squares.

BAKER'S NOTE ~

Try this recipe swapping out the apricots for equal amounts of strawberries and rhubarb.

FILLING

2 cups (380 g) ripe apricots, peeled and sliced

¼ cup (50 g) granulated sugar

1 tbsp (15 ml) lemon juice

1 tbsp (10 g) cornstarch

CRUST

1½ cups (180 g) all-purpose flour

1½ cups (125 g) old-fashioned oats, uncooked

1 cup (240 g) light brown sugar, firmly packed

½ tsp baking soda

½ tsp ground cinnamon

¼ tsp salt

¾ cup (180 g) unsalted butter, room temperature

APPLE-MAPLE BLONDIES

It's feast or famine when it comes to fruit in my house. At times, I will buy a bag of fruit, and it will be gone in an hour. Other times, I will buy the same fruit, and it sits and doesn't get touched. This is often the case with apples. When I have a few apples left over, I usually turn them into a delightful treat. Like brownies, these blondies are super simple to make. They are the perfect last-minute dessert for those unexpected mornings when your kids tell you they have to bring in a treat for their class party.

MAKES: 9 to 12 servings

Preheat the oven to 350°F (177°C). Line an 8 x 8-inch (20 x 20-cm) square baking pan with parchment paper.

To make the blondies, in a small bowl, whisk together the flour, baking soda and salt. Set it aside.

In a large mixing bowl, beat the butter, syrup and brown sugar until it's light and fluffy, about 3 minutes. Add the egg and vanilla and beat to combine them. Stir in the flour mixture. Fold in the apples.

Transfer the batter to the pan and spread it out into an even layer. Bake until a toothpick inserted into the center comes out clean, about 20 to 25 minutes. Cool the pan for 5 minutes, then transfer it to a rack to cool completely.

To make the frosting, in a medium-sized bowl, beat the cream cheese, butter and maple syrup together. Add the powdered sugar and beat until it's smooth. Spread it over the cooled apple blondies. Store the bars in an airtight container for up to 3 days.

BAKER'S NOTES ~

Make this during the summer months with fresh peaches.

Precut the apples by removing the cores and slicing them. Dip the slices in a bowl of cold water and 1 tablespoon (15 ml) of lemon juice to prevent browning. Remove the slices from the bowl and store them in a paper towel–lined container.

BLONDIES

1 cup (120 g) all-purpose flour

¼ tsp baking soda

¼ tsp salt

½ cup (120 ml) unsalted butter, melted and cooled slightly

2 tbsp (30 ml) pure maple syrup

1 cup (240 g) dark brown sugar, packed

1 large egg

1 tsp vanilla extract

2 medium-sized apples (Granny Smith, Honeycrisp or Braeburn), peeled, cored and diced

MAPLE FROSTING

4 oz (113 g) cream cheese, room temperature

2 tbsp (30 g) unsalted butter, room temperature

1 tbsp (15 ml) pure maple syrup

2 cups (240 g) powdered sugar

RASPBERRY FRANGIPANE SCONES

Whether you are making these for a family brunch or an afternoon snack, these raspberry-studded scones will be a hit. They are full of berry flavor and finish off with a light taste of buttery almond.

MAKES: 6 to 8 servings

Preheat the oven to 400°F (204°C). Line an 18 x 13-inch (46 x 33-cm) baking sheet with parchment paper or a silicone mat.

To make the scones, in a large bowl, whisk together the ½ cup (100 g) sugar, flour, baking powder and salt. Break up the almond paste into small pea-sized chunks over the flour.

Grate the butter using a box grater, then toss it into the flour mixture and stir to coat it. Alternatively, slice the cold butter and cut it into the flour mixture using a pastry cutter. Stir in the egg, almond extract and half-and-half. Gently fold in the raspberries. The dough will be wet.

On a lightly floured surface, flatten the dough out into an 8-inch (20-cm) disk. Cut the disk into 6 to 8 equal wedges. Place the wedges onto the baking sheet 2 inches (5 cm) apart. Brush the tops of each wedge with half-and-half and sprinkle them with 1 tablespoon (13 g) of sugar. Bake the scones for 20 to 25 minutes, or until they're golden brown.

Make the glaze while the scones are cooling. In a small bowl, whisk together the powdered sugar, milk and almond extract until it's smooth. Pour it over the cooled scones, then top them with sliced almonds.

BAKER'S NOTE ~

These scones are great for freezing and enjoying later. Simply wrap non-glazed scones in waxed paper and store them in an airtight container for up to three months. Defrost them at room temperature for three hours before serving. Heat them for fifteen to twenty seconds right before serving, if desired.

SCONES

½ cup (100 g) granulated sugar, plus 1 tbsp (13 g) for topping

2½ cups (300 g) all-purpose flour

3 tsp (12 g) baking powder

½ tsp salt

2 oz (60 g) almond paste

½ cup (120 g) butter, very cold or frozen

1 egg

¼ tsp almond extract

⅔ cup (160 ml) half-and-half, plus more for brushing

½ cup (65 g) fresh raspberries

GLAZE

1 cup (120 g) powdered sugar

2 tbsp (30 ml) milk

¼ tsp almond extract

Sliced almonds, for garnish

CHERRY PIE TURNOVERS

When a flaky, buttery pastry encloses a sweet, homemade cherry filling, nirvana is achieved. Just kidding. If only it was that simple! While ascending into the mental state of perfect ideal happiness requires a bit more than puff pastry and cherry filling, these instantly gratifying turnovers do not.

MAKES: 8 turnovers

In a small pan, combine the cherries, sugar and cornstarch over medium-low heat. Bring the mixture to a boil and cook until the liquid coats the back of a spoon, about 15 to 20 minutes, stirring regularly. Remove the pan from the heat and stir in the vanilla bean paste. Cool the filling to room temperature.

Preheat the oven to 400°F (204°C). Line two large baking sheets with parchment paper or foil that is lightly sprayed with nonstick cooking spray. Whisk the egg yolk and water together; set it aside.

Unfold the puff pastry sheets and trim each sheet into a square. Cut each large square into four even squares. Spoon the cherry filling into the center of each square. Brush the edges of the puff pastry squares with the egg wash. Fold the puff pastry diagonally over the mixture and seal it by pressing the edges with a fork. Place the turnovers on the baking sheets, leaving about 1 inch (2.5 cm) of space between them. Brush each entire triangle with egg wash, then sprinkle them with 1 tablespoon (13 g) of sugar.

Bake for 20 minutes, or until the turnovers are puffed and golden. Serve them warm or at room temperature.

2 cups (460 g) sweet cherries, pitted and diced

½ cup (100 g) granulated sugar

2½ tbsp (24 g) cornstarch

2 tsp (14 g) vanilla bean paste, or 1 vanilla bean, scraped

1 egg yolk

1 tsp water

2 sheets puff pastry, thawed

1 tbsp (13 g) sugar

BAKER'S NOTE

You can find vanilla bean paste online or at cooking or craft stores. Vanilla extract can be used in place of the paste or whole pods.

BLUEBERRY–WHITE CHOCOLATE OATMEAL COOKIES

There are not many recipes out there that incorporate fresh fruits into cookies. Generally, the excess water or juice from the fruits just doesn't work well. These cookies, however, are some of my personal favorites. I actually prefer to use fresh blueberries because the juices spread into the oats and flour, creating a magical cookie that is part oatmeal cookie, part blueberry muffin.

MAKES: 2 dozen cookies

Preheat the oven to 350°F (177°C). Line two cookie sheets with parchment paper or a silicon mat.

In a medium-sized bowl, combine the flour, oats, baking powder, baking soda, cinnamon and salt; set it aside.

In a separate bowl, toss the blueberries with cornstarch until they're coated; set that aside.

In a large bowl, cream the butter, shortening, granulated sugar and brown sugar until it's light and fluffy. Add the eggs and vanilla; mix well. Gradually add the flour mixture, mixing until it's just combined. Stir in the white chocolate chips and coated blueberries.

Scoop and roll the dough into 1-inch (2.5-cm) balls and place them on the prepared cookie sheet 2 inches (5 cm) apart. Gently press down on the balls to flatten them slightly.

Bake the cookies for 10 to 12 minutes or until they're golden brown. Cool them for 5 minutes on the pan, then transfer them to a cooling rack to cool completely. Store the cookies in an airtight container for up to 3 days.

2 cups (240 g) all-purpose flour

2¾ cups (225 g) rolled oats

1 tsp baking powder

1 tsp baking soda

¾ tsp ground cinnamon

½ tsp salt

1 cup (100 g) fresh blueberries, chopped in half

½ tbsp (5 g) cornstarch

½ cup (120 g) unsalted butter, softened

½ cup (100 g) vegetable shortening

¾ cup (150 g) granulated sugar

¾ cup (170 g) light brown sugar

2 large eggs

1 tsp vanilla extract

1 cup (185 g) white chocolate chips

BAKER'S NOTE ~

Make an extra batch or two of this cookie dough to enjoy later. Simply freeze the cookie dough balls on a cookie sheet. Transfer the balls to a large freezer bag and freeze them for up to three months. When you're ready to bake, place the frozen balls on a cookie sheet and let them sit at room temperature for five minutes before baking.

RASPBERRY MERINGUES

These little clouds of joy are swirled with mashed raspberries that caramelize slightly during baking. For such a simple cookie, they are delightful. The only problem with these cookies is that it is hard to stop at just one. My hips can fully attest to that.

MAKES: Approximately 30 meringues

In a small bowl, mash the raspberries and 2 teaspoons (8 g) of sugar together. If desired, strain the mixture through a fine-mesh sieve to remove the seeds. Cover and set it aside until ready to use.

Preheat the oven to 225°F (107°C). Line a baking sheet with parchment paper. Position a rack in the center of the oven.

In a large bowl, beat the egg whites, cream of tartar and salt on low speed until the mixture becomes frothy. Increase the mixer speed to high.

With the mixer speed on high, gradually add 1¼ cups (250 g) of sugar to the egg whites, 1 tablespoon (13 g) at a time. Let the sugar completely dissolve, about 15 seconds, before adding the next tablespoon. Once all of the sugar has been added, continue to beat until the mixture has doubled in volume and is thick and shiny. Using a rubber spatula, gently fold the raspberry sauce and vanilla bean paste into the meringue, just enough to where there are streaks of raspberry throughout the batter.

Pour the batter into a pastry bag fitted with a star tip and pipe little rounds onto the baking sheet. Alternatively, dollop the cookies onto the baking sheet using a spoon.

Bake the meringues for 1 hour.

¾ cup (100 g) fresh raspberries

1¼ cups (250 g) plus 2 tsp (8 g) granulated sugar, divided

6 large egg whites

¾ tsp cream of tartar

⅛ tsp salt

1 tsp vanilla bean paste, or vanilla extract

BAKER'S NOTE ∼

Meringue cookies should be stored in an airtight container and kept away from heat and moisture to maintain crispness. Avoid making these on humid days, as it adds extra moisture to the meringue and interferes with the egg whites' stability.

CHERRY DOUBLE-CHOCOLATE COOKIES

These cookies are one of the first things I make when I get my hands on some fresh cherries. While the pitting process is a bit tedious, it is so worth it in the end when you take one bite of the cherry-infused chocolate cookies. Add a bit of flaked sea salt on top, and you have one good cookie.

MAKES: 2½ dozen cookies

Preheat the oven to 350°F (177°C). Line baking sheets with parchment paper or a silicon mat.

In a medium-sized bowl, whisk together the flour, cocoa powder, baking soda and salt; set it aside.

In a separate bowl, beat the butter, shortening, granulated sugar and brown sugar until it's light and fluffy. Add the eggs and vanilla and beat on high for 3 minutes. On low speed, gradually beat in the flour mixture until it's just combined.

In a small bowl, toss the cherries with the cornstarch. Stir the cornstarch-coated cherries and chocolate chips into the cookie dough. Drop the dough in 2-tablespoon-sized (30-g) rounds, 2 inches (5 cm) apart on the baking sheets. Sprinkle them with flaky sea salt, if desired.

Bake for 9 to 10 minutes. Let the cookies cool on the pan for about 5 minutes, then transfer them to a cooling rack.

BAKER'S NOTE ∽

Typically, it is better to bake only one cookie sheet at a time. On most ovens, the heat comes from the bottom; therefore, the cookies on the bottom rack tend to burn slightly.

2¼ cups (270 g) all-purpose flour

½ cup (60 g) dark cocoa powder

1 tsp baking soda

½ tsp salt

½ cup (120 g) unsalted butter, room temperature

½ cup (100 g) butter-flavored shortening

¾ cup (150 g) granulated sugar

¾ cup (170 g) light brown sugar, packed

2 large eggs

1 tsp vanilla

1 cup (230 g) fresh cherries, pitted and diced

¼ cup (40 g) cornstarch

1½ cups (275 g) semi-sweet chocolate chips

Flaky sea salt, for garnish, optional

FROZEN SWEET CONCOCTIONS

"A recipe has no soul. You as the cook must bring soul to the recipe."

∽ *Thomas Keller*

I consider myself one of the luckiest people in the world to call Southern California my home! I can recall many a February, while the rest of the country was defrosting their frozen mittens, I was outside with a frozen margarita in my hand watching my shoeless kids flag down the ice cream truck. Along with the lovely high temps (and the high sunshine taxes), California has an endless supply of fresh produce, perfect for frozen desserts. But you don't have to live west of the Rockies to make frozen desserts, and you certainly don't have to wait for the heat to enjoy them. From the palate cleansing Watermelon-Mint Granita (page 129) to the Cranberry-Pear Ice Cream (page 141), there is a recipe for every season.

CANTALOUPE ROSÉ SORBET

On a hot summer's day, there are pretty much only two things I want for dinner: cold cantaloupe chunks and a crisp glass of rosé. So, why not combine the two? I'm quite certain that this may have been one of my best/ smartest decisions ever.

MAKES: 4 servings

In a small saucepan, combine the sugar, water and rosé over medium-high heat. Cook until the sugar has dissolved and the mixture has come to a simmer. Remove it from the heat, pour it into an airtight container and refrigerate it until cold.

Combine the rosé simple syrup, cold melon and lemon juice in a blender and puree until smooth. Pour the puree into your frozen ice cream maker and freeze it according to the machine's manufacturer instructions.

When the sorbet has thickened and is frozen, scoop it into an airtight container and freeze until it's firm. Allow the sorbet to soften at room temperature for 5 minutes before scooping.

1 cup (200 g) granulated sugar

½ cup (120 ml) water

½ cup (120 ml) dry rosé wine

4 cups (640 g) cantaloupe, cubed and chilled

2 tbsp (30 ml) fresh lemon juice

BAKER'S NOTE ~

This sorbet can be made with honeydew melons as well.

BALSAMIC-STRAWBERRY ICE CREAM

This combination may sound odd, but trust me when I say that it is absolutely fabulous. A splash of vinegar dissipates into the strawberries, enhancing their sweetness and creating a light and refreshing scoop of ice cream.

MAKES: 1 pint (230 g)

Dice the strawberries into small chunks. Toss it with 2 tablespoons (25 g) of sugar and the balsamic vinegar. Place it in a blender and pulse until it's smooth. Cover and let it marinate for 1 hour.

To make the ice cream base, in a medium-sized bowl, whisk the egg yolks and ¼ cup (50 g) of the sugar until they turn a light lemon-yellow color, about 3 or 4 minutes; set it aside.

In a medium-sized, heavy-bottomed saucepan, combine the whipping cream and milk. Cook over medium heat, whisking often, until the sugar has dissolved and the mixture is hot. Whisk the pureed strawberries into the egg yolk mixture. Temper the strawberry/egg yolk mixture by slowly adding ¼ cup (60 ml) of the hot milk mixture into the beaten egg yolks, whisking constantly until it's well blended and smooth.

Pour the mixture back into the saucepan and continue to cook over medium heat, whisking constantly, until the mixture thickens and coats the back of a spoon, about 5 minutes. Remove it from the heat and stir in the vanilla. Let the mixture cool to room temperature, then refrigerate the mixture for at least 4 hours or until cold.

Once it's cold, freeze it in an ice cream maker according to the manufacturer's instructions.

1 pint (320 g) strawberries, washed, dried and hulled

¼ cup (50 g) plus 2 tbsp (25 g) granulated sugar, divided

1½ tsp (8 ml) balsamic vinegar

3 egg yolks

2 cups (480 ml) heavy whipping cream

2 cups (480 ml) milk

1 tsp vanilla extract

BAKER'S NOTE ~

If you like fresh strawberry chunks in your ice cream, marinate an additional cup (160 g) of diced strawberries in the balsamic. Before blending, remove the cup of strawberries, cover and refrigerate them. Add them to the ice cream halfway through the churning process.

WATERMELON-MINT GRANITA

This icy treat is the best when served on a hot summer's day. It is extremely easy to make and requires a couple of visits to the freezer to break up the ice crystals. I make this recipe way too much during the summer months because I am tired of not having a legitimate reason for sticking my head in the freezer to cool off.

MAKES: 8 servings

Combine the watermelon, lime juice, sugar and mint in a blender and puree until it's smooth. Pour the puree through a fine-mesh sieve; discard the solids.

Pour the puree into a 9 x 13–inch (23 x 33–cm) baking dish and freeze it for 4 hours, scraping it with a fork every hour until the mixture is icy and flaky.

Granita can be made one day ahead of time. Scoop it into bowls or dessert glasses to serve.

½ medium seedless watermelon, rind removed and cut into 2-inch (5-cm) pieces

¼ cup (60 ml) fresh lime juice

¼ cup (50 g) granulated sugar

3 large fresh mint leaves

BAKER'S NOTE ~

Unlike other fruits, when picking a melon, you want to look for a dull-colored skin. The shinier the skin, the more underripe the fruit will be. You can also tap on the melon. If it sounds hollow inside, this indicates that the melon is ripe. Finally, if picking a cantaloupe or other melon, use your sense of smell. Sniff the part of the melon where the vine was attached. If it smells sweet and fresh, you have a winner!

ISLAND SHERBET

This is not your cheap grocery store sherbet with fake flavors and colors. No, this tropical melody will change the way you think about sherbet forever. Now, this recipe does take some time to make; however, most of that time is chilling and freezing. So the next time you want to taste the flavors of the islands or impress someone, make this! Trust me, I gained three new Facebook friends the last time I made it!

MAKES: Approximately 1¾ quarts (800 g)

Make each batch individually.

To make the pineapple-kiwi sherbet, puree the kiwis, pineapple, sugar, corn syrup and coconut milk until it's smooth. Churn it in an ice cream maker according to the manufacturer's instructions. When the sherbet is soft-serve consistency, transfer it to a container and freeze it until firm.

Make the next batch of guava-strawberry sherbet by pureeing the strawberries, pink guava puree, sugar, corn syrup and coconut milk until it's smooth, and then churn in the ice cream maker until it's a soft-serve consistency. Pour and spread it onto the pineapple-kiwi layer. Finally, repeat the steps with the final passion fruit–mango layer. Freeze it overnight. Let it stand at room temperature for 5 minutes before serving.

If not using an ice cream maker, freeze the fruit mixture purees for 15 minutes before adding the next layer. Freeze it overnight before serving.

BAKER'S NOTE ～

This sherbet can be made with almost any fruit; you'll just want to make sure that there are approximately 2 cups (300 g) of fruit to puree. Also, if your fruit is overly ripe, reduce the sugar by half, then test it before freezing. Add additional sugar if needed. Corn syrup is used in this recipe to decrease the formation of ice crystals.

PINEAPPLE-KIWI SHERBET

5 kiwis, skin removed and cut into quarters

1¾ cups (290 g) fresh pineapple chunks

¼ cup (50 g) granulated sugar

1 tbsp (15 ml) light corn syrup

1 cup (240 ml) coconut milk

GUAVA-STRAWBERRY SHERBET

½ cup (80 g) chopped strawberries

1½ cups (360 ml) pink guava puree

¼ cup (50 g) granulated sugar

1 tbsp (15 ml) light corn syrup

1 cup (240 ml) coconut milk

PASSION FRUIT–MANGO SHERBET

2 large mangos, skinned and seeds removed

1 cup (240 ml) passion fruit juice

½ cup (100 g) granulated sugar

1 tbsp (15 ml) light corn syrup

1 cup (240 ml) coconut milk

RASPBERRY-APRICOT MASCARPONE ICE CREAM

The mascarpone cheese in this ice cream recipe adds a rich creaminess that gets balanced by fresh apricots and raspberries. It's the Versace of ice creams. And since I can't afford a real Versace piece, I'll settle for some high-class ice cream.

MAKES: 2 pints (460 g)

In a saucepan over medium heat, cook the apricots with ¼ cup (50 g) of the sugar until the fruit is tender, about 10 minutes. Set it aside.

In a small pot, bring the cream and milk to a simmer, then remove it from the heat and stir in the salt and vanilla.

In a separate bowl, whisk the egg yolks and the remaining sugar until the mixture is a pale yellow. Temper the egg mixture by slowly pouring one-third of the hot cream into the egg mixture while whisking briskly. Pour the tempered egg mixture back into the pot with the remaining cream, whisking constantly. Return the pot to medium-low heat and cook, continuously stirring, until the mixture is thick enough to coat the back of the spoon. Strain it into a bowl through a fine-mesh sieve. Whisk the mascarpone into the hot ice cream base. Stir in the apricots. Cool the mixture to room temperature. Cover and chill the custard for at least 4 hours or preferably overnight.

Once it's cold, churn the custard in an ice cream machine according to the manufacturer's instructions. Halfway through the churning process, add the fresh raspberries. Serve the ice cream directly from the machine for delicious soft serve, or store it in the freezer until needed. If you're freezing it, allow the ice cream to thaw at room temperature for 5 minutes before scooping.

1½ lb (680 g) apricots, pitted and coarsely chopped

¼ cup (50 g) plus ⅔ cup (130 g) granulated sugar, divided

2 cups (480 ml) heavy cream

1 cup (240 ml) whole milk

⅛ tsp salt

1 tsp vanilla extract

6 large egg yolks

1 cup (225 g) fresh mascarpone cheese

2 pints (520 g) fresh raspberries

BAKER'S NOTE ~

The addition of mascarpone in the ice cream base gives a very creamy, rich flavor that would pair well with any fruit.

POMEGRANATE-ALMOND CHAMPAGNE SORBET

Ring in the New Year with a scoop of this delectably fresh sorbet. We also love making it and serving it as a palate cleanser or light dessert during the holidays.

MAKES: 1 pint (230 g)

Combine the almond champagne, sugar and light corn syrup in a small saucepan over medium-high heat. Bring the mixture to a boil, stirring occasionally, then remove it from the heat. Whisk in the pomegranate juice.

Place the mixture in a bowl, cover and refrigerate it for 4 hours. If it's needed sooner, freeze the mixture for 2 hours.

When the mixture is chilled, churn it in an ice cream maker according to the manufacturer's instructions.

Serve immediately or store it in an airtight container in the freezer to enjoy later. Serve the sorbet with a dollop of whipped cream, crushed amaretti cookies and a few pomegranate arils, if desired.

1½ cups (360 ml) almond champagne

¾ cup (150 g) granulated sugar

1 tbsp (15 ml) light corn syrup

2 cups (480 ml) pomegranate juice

Whipped cream, for garnish

Crushed amaretti cookies, for garnish

Pomegranate arils, for garnish, optional

BAKER'S NOTE ⌒

While churning in an ice cream maker produces a creamier sorbet, the mixture can also be directly frozen in an airtight container for four to six hours. Let it thaw a few minutes before scooping.

TROPICAL MANGO POPSICLES

Sweet, juicy mango, pineapple and coconut milk are an unbeatably refreshing combo and quite a vibrant dessert when combined with speckled dragon fruit and delicious kiwi. It's practically art on a stick! This all-natural dessert is a delicious way to cool off without worry. Unless of course you follow my directions for the adult version, and I highly recommend that you do. Just make sure to label them properly!

MAKES: 12 popsicles

Puree the mangos, pineapple juice and coconut milk until it's smooth. Pour the puree into each mold cavity or cup, two-thirds full. Insert the kiwi slices and dragon fruit into each cavity. Top them with additional puree, if necessary.

Cover the mold with foil and make a small incision in the center of each cavity. Insert a popsicle stick through each incision one-third of the way into the popsicle. Freeze them for 4 hours.

To remove them from the mold, quickly dip the mold into hot water and remove the popsicles.

2 large mangos, peeled and cored

1½ cups (360 ml) pineapple juice

½ cup (120 ml) coconut milk

4 large kiwis, peeled and sliced

1 large dragon fruit, peeled and sliced

BAKER'S NOTES

Special equipment needed: 12 popsicle molds or paper cups and popsicle sticks

For an adult version, replace the coconut milk with vodka and add 2 tablespoons (30 ml) of simple syrup.

BLACKBERRY VACHERIN

This impressive French dessert is made up of crushed meringues, ice cream, berries and whipped cream. It is one of my husband's favorite desserts, as it was served to him on many occasions growing up. It is a wonderful summer recipe, because there is no cooking involved!

MAKES: 10 to 12 servings

Line an 8-inch (20-cm) springform pan with parchment paper or plastic wrap.

Remove the ice cream from the freezer to soften for about 10 minutes. Once soft, put it into a large bowl and stir in the blackberries. Add 1 cup (100 g) of the crushed meringues to the bottom of the lined springform pan. Scoop one-third of the ice cream over the crushed meringues. Repeat the layers two more times. Freeze the *vacherin* for 1 hour or until it's solid.

Remove the cake right before serving. Using an electric mixer, beat the heavy cream and powdered sugar until stiff peaks form. Top the vacherin with the whipped cream, blackberries and a sprinkle of chopped pistachios.

1½ quarts (865 g) vanilla bean ice cream, softened

2 cups (290 g) blackberries, washed and dried, plus more for garnish

3 cups (300 g) crushed meringues, homemade or store-bought, divided

1 cup (240 ml) heavy whipping cream

1 tbsp (8 g) powdered sugar

⅓ cup (35 g) pistachios, finely chopped, for garnish

BAKER'S NOTE ～

Substitute any berry for the blackberries in this recipe. For an extra-special dessert, make the cake with Raspberry-Apricot Mascarpone Ice Cream (page 133). This recipe can also be halved and made in a lined loaf pan.

CRANBERRY-PEAR ICE CREAM

Just because it's cold out doesn't mean that you can't have a delicious bowl of ice cream! With these warm cranberry and pear flavors, you'll still be tasting the holidays, but in a different way. Enjoy a scoop next to the fire or on top of a warm slice of Fall's Best Apple-Pear Pie (page 81).

MAKES: 1½ pints (344 g)

In a heavy saucepan set over medium heat, bring the cranberries, pears, ⅓ cup (70 g) of sugar, cinnamon and nutmeg to a simmer. Continue to cook for approximately 10 minutes, or until the cranberries have popped and the pear chunks are soft. Remove it from the heat and set it aside to cool. Once cooled, cover and refrigerate it until you're ready to churn it with the ice cream base.

In a small pot, bring the cream, milk, vanilla bean pod and scraped seeds and cinnamon stick to a simmer, then remove the pan from the heat and stir in the salt; let it sit for 10 minutes.

In a separate bowl, whisk the egg yolks and the remaining ⅔ cup (130 g) sugar until the mixture is a pale yellow. Remove and discard the vanilla bean pod and cinnamon stick from the cream. Temper the egg mixture by slowly pouring one-third of the hot cream into the egg mixture while whisking briskly. Pour the tempered egg mixture back into the pot with the remaining cream, whisking constantly. Return the pot to medium-low heat and cook, while continuously stirring, until the mixture is thick enough to coat the back of the spoon. Strain it through a fine-mesh sieve into a bowl.

Cover and chill the ice cream base for at least 4 hours or preferably overnight.

Once it's cold, churn the ice cream base in an ice cream machine according to the manufacturer's instructions. Halfway through the churning process, pour in the chilled cranberry-pear compote. Serve the ice cream directly from the machine for delicious soft serve, or store it in the freezer until it's needed. If you're freezing it, allow the ice cream to thaw at room temperature for 5 minutes before scooping.

1 lb (450 g) fresh cranberries

3 pears, cored and diced

1 cup (200 g) granulated sugar, divided

1 tsp ground cinnamon

¼ tsp ground nutmeg

2 cups (480 ml) heavy cream

1 cup (240 ml) whole milk

1 vanilla bean, sliced open and seeds scraped

1 cinnamon stick

⅛ tsp salt

6 large egg yolks

BAKER'S NOTE ∼

Add a tablespoon (15 ml) of brandy or orange zest (10 g) to the cranberry compote after cooking.

RETRO-MODERN DELIGHTS

"Drama is very important in life: You have to come on with a bang. You never want to go out with a whimper. Everything can have drama if it's done right. Even a pancake."

Julia Child

I'm not sure when my obsession with pulverizing fruit came about, but it has resulted in some delicious desserts that are tantalizingly smooth like Bruno Mars! The idea of curd, as in the infamous lemon curd, may bring about visions of large floral dresses, Earl Grey and the word, "indubitably." I have made it my mission to bring curd back in all its flavorful, retro-modern, sexy glory!

Pureed desserts are packed with tangy sweetness and are incredibly simple to make but scream effort, sophistication and right-nowness.

FRUIT CURD BASE

I almost wrote an entire book on fruit curds; that's how much I love them. My husband always jokes when I come home with an abundance of fruit because he knows that the top half of the fridge will soon be filled with multiple jars of fresh curd. This is my base recipe that works with pretty much every fruit I have used.

MAKES: About 1¼ cups (305 g)

In a heavy-bottomed, medium-sized pot, whisk together the sugar and eggs until it's pale yellow in color. Whisk in the juice and zest, if using. Place the pot over medium heat and whisk constantly until the curd is thick enough to coat the back of a spoon, about 5 to 7 minutes. Stir in the butter. Strain the curd through a fine-mesh sieve and pour it into a jar or a bowl. Cover it with a lid or plastic wrap and refrigerate it for at least 2 hours or up to 1 week.

Use the curd to fill cakes, cupcakes, French *macarons* or just simply eat with a spoon.

½ cup (100 g) granulated sugar

3 large eggs

½ cup (120 ml) fresh citrus juice or fruit puree

2 tsp (6 g) finely grated zest, if making a citrus curd

6 tbsp (80 g) unsalted butter, cut into slices

> **BAKER'S NOTE** ～
>
> *Combine the fruits to make a tasty concoction, such as passion fruit–mango, razzleberry or triple citrus. For very ripe fruit or sweet fruit, reduce the sugar to ¼ cup (50 g) or add a tablespoon (15 ml) of fresh lemon juice.*

BLUEBERRY MOUSSE

Served in small, individual glasses, this Blueberry Mousse portrays itself as being a delicate, hard-to-make dessert. The truth is that although it looks fancy, it is incredibly easy to make and can be made up to two days ahead of time. Serve it at your next summer luncheon or dinner party for a delicious dessert that will get rave reviews. The blueberries in this recipe can be replaced with any berry in the same quantity. It is also delicious during the holidays with cranberries and an additional ½ cup (100 g) of sugar.

MAKES: 4 servings

In a small bowl, combine the cold water and gelatin; set it aside.

In a medium-sized saucepan, combine the blueberries, sugar and lime juice. Cook on medium heat until the berries begin to pop, about 6 to 8 minutes. Remove it from the heat and whisk in the gelatin until it's completely dissolved. Let the mixture come to room temperature. Once the blueberry mixture is no longer warm, place it in a blender and puree until smooth.

Beat the heavy whipping cream on high until stiff peaks form. Using a rubber spatula, gently fold the lime zest and cooled blueberry sauce into the cream.

If you're serving that day, pour it into serving cups and refrigerate it for 90 minutes before serving. If you're making it in advance, pour the mousse into an airtight container with a lid and refrigerate them until you're ready to serve. Garnish them with whipped cream, fresh blueberries and mint.

2 tbsp (30 ml) cold water

1½ tsp (7 g) powdered gelatin

2 cups (200 g) fresh blueberries, plus more for garnish

½ cup (100 g) granulated sugar

2 tbsp (30 ml) lime juice

2 cups (480 ml) heavy whipping cream

1 tbsp (10 g) lime zest

Whipped cream, for garnish

Mint sprigs, for garnish

BAKER'S NOTE ∽

How to Store Berries

Rinse berries with a tablespoon (15 ml) of apple cider vinegar to a cup (240 ml) of cold water. Then, rinse them again and let them air-dry for about 20 minutes. Store the berries in a paper towel–lined bowl or container in the refrigerator.

POMEGRANATE PANNA COTTA

Who would have thought that some milk, cream and gelatin would transform into molded perfection? I always had my doubts about this dessert, as I am not a huge fan of milk. But when I had this pomegranate-infused dessert for the first time in Italy, I just about fell to my knees. The lesson here is to not hold back on trying new things; you may be pleasantly surprised by the outcome!

MAKES: 8 servings

To make the pomegranate *gelée*, sprinkle the gelatin over 2 tablespoons (30 ml) of the pomegranate juice and mix well. Set it aside.

Combine the sparkling wine and sugar in a small saucepan over medium-high heat. Cook until the sugar has dissolved. Add the remaining pomegranate juice and bring the mixture to a simmer; remove it from the heat. Add the gelatin mixture and stir until it's completely dissolved. Divide the gelatin evenly in the molds. Freeze them for 20 minutes or refrigerate them for 1 hour until the gelée has set.

To make the panna cotta, sprinkle the gelatin over the water in a small microwave-safe bowl; set it aside until it's soft.

In a medium-sized saucepan set over medium heat, combine the heavy cream, milk, sugar and vanilla bean pod and seeds; bring it to a boil. Once it's boiling, remove the pan from the heat. Microwave the gelatin for 10 to 15 seconds until it's runny. Whisk the gelatin mixture into the hot cream mixture. Carefully pour the hot mixture evenly over the chilled fruit gelée in the molds; let sit at room temperature until they're no longer hot. Once the molds have cooled down, cover and refrigerate them for at least 6 hours.

BAKER'S NOTES ∽

Special equipment needed: 8 (4-oz [120-ml]) jars/ramekins/panna cotta molds

The reason you need a significant amount more gelatin in the puree than in the panna cotta is because the pomegranate juice is so acidic it requires more gelatin to set.

POMEGRANATE GELÉE

1 (¼-oz [7-g]) package unflavored powdered gelatin

½ cup (120 ml) pomegranate juice, divided

½ cup (120 ml) sparkling white wine or sparkling grape juice

1½ tbsp (20 g) granulated sugar

PANNA COTTA

1 tbsp (14 g) unflavored powdered gelatin, divided

2 tbsp (30 ml) water

2 cups (480 ml) heavy cream

1 cup (240 ml) whole milk

⅓ cup (70 g) granulated sugar

1 vanilla bean pod, sliced in half and seeds scraped

CARAMEL–PASSION FRUIT POT *de* CRÈME

These little jars of silky smooth custard are packed with delicious flavor. The tart passion fruit pairs perfectly with the caramel undertones. Although not difficult, this recipe does require a few steps and some extra dishes. But like my husband says, "If it was easy, everyone would do it!" Some things, especially these mini cups of joy, are worth the trouble.

MAKES: 6 servings

Cut each passion fruit in half and scoop out the pulp and seeds into a fine-mesh sieve over a bowl. Rub the fruit through the sieve, discarding the seeds. Set the juice aside.

Preheat the oven to 325°F (163°C).

In a heavy-bottomed saucepan, combine the passion fruit juice, heavy cream and salt over medium-low heat. Cook until the cream begins to simmer. Once simmering, remove the pan from the heat.

Make the caramel by combining ¾ cup (150 g) of the sugar and 6 tablespoons (90 ml) water in a small saucepan over medium heat. Cook until the sugar has dissolved and the mixture is an amber color, stirring constantly for 4 to 5 minutes. Watch carefully to avoid burning. Remove the caramel from the heat and carefully pour it into the hot cream mixture.

In a large bowl, whisk the egg yolks and the remaining ¼ cup (50 g) sugar until it's light and pale. Temper the egg yolk mixture by gradually adding in the passion fruit/caramel cream mixture while whisking.

Evenly pour the custard mixture into six ¾-cup (180-ml) custard jars. Cover each with foil. Place the jars into a large pan and add enough hot water to come halfway up the sides of the jars. Bake for 50 to 55 minutes or until the custards are set but the centers move slightly when shaken. Remove the foil and custards from the pan. If not serving them warm, cool them to room temperature, then chill the custards for at least 3 hours or up to 2 days. Serve with whipped cream and a drizzle of caramel sauce.

7–9 fresh passion fruits

1½ cups (360 ml) heavy cream

¼ tsp salt

1 cup (200 g) granulated sugar, divided

6 tbsp (90 ml) water

5 large egg yolks

Whipped cream, for garnish

Caramel sauce, for garnish

BAKER'S NOTES ⁓

Special equipment needed: 6 (¾-cup [180-ml]) jars or ramekins

These are delicious served with an extra drizzle of caramel sauce. For a homemade version, refer to the Bananas Foster Cake (page 40).

BANANA-CHOCOLATE POT *de* CRÈME *with* COGNAC SAUCE

This is probably one of the most decadent desserts in this book. While testing the recipe, I served this to my French friend. You know when someone who has been raised on the crème de la crème of desserts falls to their knees after one bite, you have one hell of a good dessert on your hands.

MAKES: 6 to 8 servings

Preheat the oven to 325°F (163°C).

To make the banana-chocolate crème, bring the cream to a simmer in a heavy-bottomed, medium-sized saucepan over medium heat. Once it's simmering, remove it from the heat and add the chocolate chunks. Let it sit for 3 minutes, then whisk until the chocolate has melted and is smooth.

In a large bowl, whisk the egg yolks and sugar until it's light and pale. Whisk in the mashed banana. Temper the egg yolk mixture by slowly whisking the hot chocolate mixture into the eggs. Stir in the cognac, if using.

Evenly pour the custard mixture into six ¾-cup (180-ml) custard cups. Cover each with foil. Place the cups into a large pan and add enough hot water to come halfway up the sides of the cups. Bake for 50 to 55 minutes or until the custards are set but the centers move slightly when shaken. Remove the foil and custards from the pan. If you're not serving them warm, chill the custards for at least 3 hours or up to 2 days. Reheat them in the microwave for 20 seconds or until warm, if desired.

To make the cognac caramel sauce, combine the butter, brown sugar and heavy cream in a small saucepan over medium heat. Bring the mixture to a simmer, stirring constantly. Cook until the sauce coats the back of a spoon, about 6 to 8 minutes. Remove it from the heat and stir in the cognac. Allow it to cool for 10 minutes, then transfer the sauce to an airtight container. Refrigerate it until you're ready to serve or up to 2 weeks.

To make the whipped cream, beat the heavy whipping cream, powdered sugar and vanilla on high until stiff peaks form. Pipe or dollop it onto the warm or chilled custards, then drizzle them with the cognac caramel sauce.

BANANA-CHOCOLATE CRÈME

2½ cups (600 ml) heavy cream

7 oz (200 g) bittersweet (not unsweetened) or semisweet chocolate, chopped

6 large egg yolks

¼ cup (50 g) granulated sugar

¼ cup (60 g) bananas, mashed until smooth

2 tbsp (30 ml) cognac, optional

COGNAC CARAMEL SAUCE

¼ cup (60 g) unsalted butter

½ cup (120 g) dark brown sugar

¼ cup (60 ml) heavy cream

2 tbsp (30 ml) cognac

WHIPPED CREAM

1 cup (240 ml) heavy whipping cream

1 tbsp (8 g) powdered sugar

1 tsp vanilla extract

PASSION FRUIT PASTRY CREAM

The creaminess from the custard combined with the tart flavors of passion fruit are a match made in tropical heaven. While this is a great base recipe for many desserts, I often prefer to simply enjoy it with a spoon.

MAKES: 2½ cups (710 g)

Cut each passion fruit in half and scoop out the pulp and seeds into a fine-mesh sieve over a bowl. Rub the pulp through the sieve, discarding the seeds. Set the juice aside.

In a heavy-bottomed saucepan, combine the milk and cream over medium-low heat. Cook until the milk begins to simmer. Do not let it boil. Stir in the passion fruit juice.

In a separate bowl, whisk together the egg yolks and sugar until the sugar is dissolved and the mixture is a pale yellow. Add the cornstarch and whisk vigorously until no lumps remain. Temper the egg yolk mixture by slowly adding ¼ cup (60 ml) of the milk mixture to the egg yolk mixture while whisking continuously. Repeat with ¼ cup (60 ml) of the milk mixture. Pour the egg/milk mixture back into the remaining simmering milk through a fine-mesh sieve. Continue cooking and stirring the pastry cream until the mixture has thickened and coats the back of the spoon, about 4 minutes. Stir in the butter.

Pour the mixture into a storage container and place a piece of plastic wrap directly on top of the custard, making sure that the wrap touches the cream so it does not develop a "skin." Refrigerate until it's cold and use it as a filling for a pie, éclairs, doughnuts or our Tropical Fruit Trifle (page 45).

6–7 passion fruits

1½ cups (360 ml) whole milk

½ cup (120 ml) heavy cream

6 large egg yolks

⅔ cup (130 g) granulated sugar

3½ tbsp (35 g) cornstarch

1 tbsp (15 g) salted butter

> **BAKER'S NOTE**
>
> *This is a base recipe for most pastry creams. If you are looking to make another fruity flavor, simply replace the passion fruit with ½ cup (120 ml) of fruit puree. Guava makes an amazing pastry cream too.*

ACKNOWLEDGMENTS

There is a pivotal moment in one's life where you learn who your real friends and cheerleaders are. Through the process of writing this book, I came to realize that I have way more supporters than I ever thought I had. And that, my friends, is an amazing feeling.

To my friends who swooped in to help test recipes, edit and even help occupy my kids, you are priceless.

To my family for being the best support tribe, thank you! Mom and Dad, thank you for helping me with some of the wording in the book. Your extensive vocabulary has helped me from high school until now!

Thank you to my grandmother, who has always been my number one supporter. Your encouragement and prayers mean the world to me!

Thank you to my wonderful children, who have more refined palates than any other children I know. Thank you for all of your honest reviews of the recipes and for putting up with this chaos. I can't wait to have some quality family time with each of you!

And of course, a thank you to my incredibly amazing husband. Despite the whirlwind of life going on around us, you pushed me to take on this project and helped me with everything to the very sleepless end. Thank you for always being my biggest cheerleader and my rock.

A huge thank you to my editor and publisher at Page Street Publishing. This has been an incredible opportunity that has pushed me to grow in so many ways!

Finally, thank you to all of The Seaside Baker fans. I love every minute of what I do because of you!

ABOUT THE AUTHOR

Jackie Bruchez created the blog The Seaside Baker six years ago in an effort to find a fun, creative outlet. It quickly became her passion and her full-time business. She and her family love to garden, visit "you-pick" farms and hit the farmers' market every weekend. After harvesting or buying enough produce to feed an army, she and her family return home and turn their bounty into something delectable to share. Jackie loves to entertain and uses good food as a way to show she cares. If Jackie is not in the kitchen, you can find her on the computer looking for and/or booking her next big adventure. Her family learned early on that travel was in her blood and has since caught the "bug." The Seaside Baker has been featured many times on *Huffington Post*, Buzzfeed and many other online newspapers. Her work has also appeared in the Macy's/The Knot Summer wedding edition and on many brand websites. Last year, Jackie won Judge's Choice in the Grilled Cheese Sandwich competition. She's pretty confident in her entry for next year, considering her family had been living off of grilled cheese sandwiches and fruit desserts while she wrote this book.

INDEX